The Emperor Is Naked

Understanding the second US Civil War under Trump

DAVE ROMAIN

Printed by:
Globexports CARICOM Inc.

Printed in the Canada

First Printing Edition, 2021
ISBN 978-1-9992983-5-7

Table of Contents

The Emperor Is Naked

About the Author v

Disclaimer vi

Chapter One 1

RISE OF THE SERPENT..1

Newspapers And Magazines Supporting Trump's White
SUPREMACY AGENDA...3

TALK RADIO SUPPORTING TRUMP'S WHITE SUPREMACY
AGENDA 3

MEDIA WATCHDOGS SUPPORTING TRUMP'S WHITE
SUPREMACY AGENDA...4

PERSONALITIES SUPPORTING TRUMP'S WHITE
SUPREMACY AGENDA...4

JOURNALIST'S SUPPORTING TRUMP'S WHITE
SUPREMACY AGENDA...5

WHAT CAN WE TAKE AWAY FROM THIS? 7

MAGA: US CIVIL WAR II 8

BLACK LIVES MATTER 12

Chapter two..23

PRECEDENCE FOR SLAVERY 23

THE LAW OF DISCOVERY 29

WHITE SUPREMACISTS EXPERIMENT ON HUMANS........33

WHY AMERICANS UPHOLD WHITE SUPREMACY 38

ROMAN CIVIL LAW 43
Chapter three..51

DESTROYING THE LIE...51

WHITE SUPREMACY'S FAILURE...................................53
A TRUTH CONCERNING EXISTENCE 59
Chapter FOUR 72

LASTING TRUTHS 72

Chapter FIVE...88

TRUMP GOES OFF THE RESERVATION 89

Chapter SIX 109

THE UNPRESIDENTIAL PRESIDENT...........................110

BIBLIOGRAPHY 116

About the Author

Two swindlers arrive at the capital city of an emperor who spends lavishly on clothing at the expense of state matters. Posing as weavers, they offer to supply him with magnificent clothes that are invisible to those who are stupid or incompetent. The emperor hires them, and they set up looms and go to work. A succession of officials, and then the emperor himself, visit them to check their progress. Each sees that the looms are empty but pretends otherwise to avoid being thought a fool. Finally, the weavers report that the emperor's suit is finished. They mime dressing him and he sets off in a procession before the whole city. The townsfolk uncomfortably go along with the pretense, not wanting to appear inept or stupid, until a child blurts out that the emperor is wearing nothing at all. The people then realize that everyone has been fooled. Although startled, the emperor continues the procession, walking more proudly than ever. The story is about something widely accepted as true due to an unwillingness of the general population to criticize it or be seen as going against popular opinion. This is the situation of president Donald J. Trump and ad his 75,000,000 US followers. Not one of Trump's followers is disposed to see the truth: That their leader Donald J. Trump is clearly insane. Everything about Trump is either a failed proposition or a lie. They are incapable   and or unwilling to admit that the man who styles himself a billionaire s not; intelligent is a fool; styles himself a statesman is a bully; and adult is a child and moreover sane; is clearly insane and living in his own fantasy-world. But a spiritual child, meaning myself, will point out the obvious to so many swindled by white supremacy, and self-delusion, "The emperor is naked! "President Donald J. Trump is insane!"

DISCLAIMER

I am not an MD, psychologist or psychiatrist. However, what I am is a person who recognizes crazy when I see it. And what I saw in the Trump presidency, qualifies. My current wife's granddaughter, Sariyah, when she was just four years old often engaged in imaginary play in her own world, she called Crystal City. One day, I had a very enlightening conversation with her. She tried to get me to share her imaginary reality but, on this occasion, I was not disposed to humor her whims so I said to her, "You are aware that your Crystal City is imaginary. Aren't you?" She thought about what I said for a moment and then replied, "You deal with reality and I will deal with the imaginary". I replied, "Alright!" and so it was. That evening, I learned that she did know the difference between real and imaginary, but she prefers imaginary to real from time to time. Donald Trump is not 4 years old, but he shows a decided leaning to the world of his imagination, most of the times. However, unlike my wife's granddaughter he shows no evidence of making a fine distinction between his imaginary world and reality. Moreover, just like my wife's granddaughter who wished me to play in her imaginary world, he has asked the US population of over 330,000,000 out of which according to election polls just about 75,000,000 has accepted. Some the title of this book is more than appropriate it is frightening.

AUTHOR NAME

Dave Romain

RISE OF THE SERPENT

If you are Afrimerican why would you vote for Trump? What could make you support a right-wing Klan-loving, African-hating, white supremacist? There are self-hating people in just about every group, but undoubtedly, there are more self-hating Afrimericans in the US who blindly support their enemies to their detriment because of The Stockholm syndrome and Post Traumatic Slave Syndrome. Trump exhibited a pattern of discrimination towards his Afrimerican tenants and called for draconian punitive measures in the Central Park Five case concerning five exonerated Afrimerican teens. He boasted and made a public show of questioning Barack Obama's citizenship, but to date will not release his income tax returns like every other president under the law. Trump's impeachment report, written by Mueller, is a useless document because his attorney General William Barr heavily redacted it on his behalf. Trump told Afrimerican lawmakers to "go back where they came from". He defends white terrorism, Klan confederate monuments, refers to BLM as a "terrorist organization" and has only praise for the Klan, Skinheads, and white supremacists. He refers to African Nations as "shit hole countries", and to the Alt-Right as "very fine people". On August 2016, to Afrimerican voters Trump lied and said, "You're living in poverty, your schools are no good, you have no jobs, 58% of your youth is unemployed. What the hell do you have to lose?" According to the Bureau of Labor Statistics, the unemployment rate for young Afrimericans at that time was only 19.2%. In October 2016 he claimed, "Our inner cities are a disaster. You get shot walking to the store. They have no education. They have no jobs." He thinks Afrimericans are uneducated and criticizes them at every turn. He tweeted "LeBron James was just interviewed by the dumbest man on television, Don Lemon. He made LeBron look smart, which isn't easy to do. I like Mike!" In June 2019 after Elijah Cummings criticized the conditions of immigrant detention centers at the U.S.-Mexico border, Trump called the Maryland congressman's district which is a majority Afrimerican a "disgusting, rat, and rodent infested mess" and "far worse and more dangerous" than the detention centers. And in October 2019 he characterized his impeachment as a lynching, which is the systemic murders of Afrimericans following the Civil War. The NAACP states that there were 4,743 recorded lynchings between 1882 and 1968. Roughly three-quarters of the victims were African American, with lynchings used as a weapon to terrorize the Afrimerican community. In May 2020 venting his displeasure at the anti-racism protests around the country following the police killing of the defenseless George Floyd and numerous other unarmed Afrimericans, Trump tweeted, "These THUGS are dishonoring the memory of George Floyd, and I won't let that happen. Just spoke to Governor Tim Walz and told him that the Military is with him all the way. Any difficulty and we will assume control but, when the looting starts, the shooting starts." In June 2020 He called anti-racism protesters "looters, thugs" and "other forms of lowlife and scum." Of course, none of this stops Afrimerican bootlickers from groveling at this excuse for a human being's feet.

Newspapers And Magazines Supporting Trump's White SUPREMACY AGENDA

American Thinker; Breitbart; Canada Free Press; Catholic Edition; Catholic News; Service City Journal; CNS News; Conservative News and Views; Conservative Review; Drudge Report; Fox News; Free Republic; Gateway Pundit; Hot Air; Human Events; Investor's Business Daily; LifeNews.com; Life Site; News Memeorandum.com; Military Times; National Catholic Reporter; National Review Online; News Revolt; News busters; News Max One; News Now.com; Pajamas Media; Red State; Ricochet Right Wing News; RIGHTNETWORK; Spero News; The Blaze; The Daily Caller; The Hill; The New Media Journal; Town Hall; TrevorLoudon.com; TruthRevolt.org; United Press International; America's Survival; Voice of America; Washington Examiner; Washington Free Beacon; Washington Times; Whitehousedossier.com; World Net Daily.

TALK RADIO SUPPORTING TRUMP'S WHITE SUPREMACY AGENDA

Rush Limbaugh; Glenn Beck; Sean Hannity; Mark Levin; Michael Savage; Laura Ingraham; Neal Boortz; Hugh Hewitt; Dana Loesch; Kevin Jackson; G. Gordon Liddy; Dennis Prager; Monica Crowley; Michael Reagan; Phyllis Schlafly; Tammy Bruce; Herman Cain; Dennis Miller; Dr. Laura Schlessinger; Mark Davis; Greg Garrison; Steve Malzberg; Tom Sullivan; Michael Medved; Howie Carr; Jay Severin; Mike Rosen; Jay Sekulow; Mike McConnell; Chris Baker; Cal Thomas; Michael Berry; Lee Rodgers; Ben Shapiro; John Gibson; Mancow Muller; Mike Gallagher; Roger Hedgecock; Bill Cunningham; Lars Larson; Curtis Sliwa; Ed Morrissey; Michael Koolidge; Scott Hennen; Larry Elder; Lou Dobbs; Michael Graham; Andrew Wilkow; Rusty Humphries; Tony Katz; Jordan Sekulow; Andrea Shea King; Rick Amato; Mike Church; The Victory Sessions.

MEDIA WATCHDOGS SUPPORTING TRUMP'S WHITE SUPREMACY AGENDA

Accuracy in Media; American Decency Association; Center for Media and Public Affairs; Culture and Media Institute; Family Research Council; Media Fairness; Caucus Media Research Center; Media Trackers; Morality in Media; Movie guide; News Busters; Parents Television Council; Projectveritas.com; Sunlight Foundation; Times Watch; True The Vote; Watchdog.org

PERSONALITIES SUPPORTING TRUMP'S WHITE SUPREMACY AGENDA

Ginni Thomas (Wife of Chief Justice Clarence Thomas); Judge Jeanine Pirro; Bill O'Reilly; Michael Reagan; Scott Rasmussen; Grover Norquist; Chris Wallace; Brit Hume; Ann Coulter; Sarah Palin; Elizabeth Hasslebeck; Charles Krauthammer; Patrick J. Buchanan; Megyn Kelly; Dana Perino; Dick Morris; Bernie Goldberg; Bill Kristol; Oliver North; Sean Hannity; Glenn Beck; Steve Forbes; James Dobson; Andrew Napolitano; Dr. Laura Schlessinger; Lou Dobbs; David Limbaugh; Greg Gutfeld; Karl Rove; Mike Huckabee; S.E. Cupp; John Stossel; Bret Baier; Brent Bozell; Lynne Cheney; Fred Barnes; Neil Cavuto; John Bolton; Larry Kudlow; Dennis Miller; Jedediah Bila; Ralph Reed; Tony Perkins; Bill Bennett; Ken Blackwell; Kimberly Guilfoyle; Dinesh D'Souza; Gerald Celente; Frank Luntz; Rick Santelli; Ari Fleischer; Michael Barone; Daniel Pipes; Ann Barnhardt; Stuart Varney; Rudolf Giuliani.

JOURNALIST'S SUPPORTING TRUMP'S WHITE SUPREMACY AGENDA

Gary Bauer; Tucker Carlson; Timothy P. Carney; Jerome Corsi; Steven Crowder; Ed Driscoll; Matt Drudge; Nina Easton; Erick Erickson; Joseph Farah; Mike Flynn; Patrick Frey; John H. Fund; Major Garrett; Pamela Geller; Jim Geraghty; Hannah Giles; Jonah Goldberg; Mary Katharine Ham; Peter Hitchens; David Horowitz; Cliff Kincaid; Aaron Klein; Stanley Kurtz; Dana Loesch; Michelle Malkin; Jason Mattera; Stacy McCain; John Nolte; James O'Keefe; Katie Pavlich; Joel Pollak; Dan Riehl; James S. Robbins; Lila Rose; Debbie Schlussel; Peter Schweizer; Ben Shapiro; Thomas Sowell; Jill Stanek; Todd Starnes; Mark Steyn; Andrea Tantaros; James Taranto; Cal Thomas; Eugene Volokh; Byron York.

According to Slate staff writer Mark Joseph Stern --On the morning of 6th January, 2021 Ginni Thomas—wife of Supreme Court Justice Clarence Thomas—endorsed the protest on her social media account demanding that Congress overturn the election, then sent her "LOVE" to the demonstrators who subsequently stormed the Capitol Building. According to ABC News "The wife of Supreme Court Justice Clarence Thomas used her Facebook page to amplify unsubstantiated claims of Joe Biden corruption. On 6th January, 2021, Ginni Thomas, conservative activist, asked her more than 10,000 followers to consider sharing a link focused on the alleged corruption of President Elect Joe Biden and Hunter Biden, his son, as well as claims that social media companies are censoring reports about the Bidens". In a tirade delivered before the insurrection president Trump incited the crowd with these words, "You'll never take back our country with weakness. You have to show strength and you have to be strong.... We're going to walk down Pennsylvania Avenue, ... and we're going to the Capitol... and we're going to try [to] give our Republicans... the kind of pride and boldness that they need to take back our country." On several videos members of the capitol Hill police-force are seen taking selfies with the thugs storming the Capitol Building and opening crowd barriers for the crowd. The Capitol Hill Police Chief claims that he made six (6) requests to his superiors for more officer support and they turned him down. Yet, he is the only one asked to resign. What about his superiors who turned him down? Why is no one looking into their conduct and subsequent decision not to give the chief more personnel which directly contributed to the chief and his officers being overwhelmed by the crowd. Further, Rudolf Giuliani accompanied by professor John Eastman emboldened the crowd with these words, "Everything that has been outlined for today is perfectly legal..."

WHAT CAN WE TAKE AWAY FROM THIS?

From the above we may deduce that the January 6th US Insurrection was just the tip of the iceberg. Many influential persons were involved in the insurrection to include 45th president Donald John Trump, Ginni Thomas, Rudolf Giuliani, John Eastman, a plethora of Republican government officials, Capitol Hill Police upper echelons who turned down Capitol Hill police chief Jon Homan's 6 requests for more officer support. Further, we may deduce that for influential lawyers connected to the US president, there is no authority over lawyers worth the paper their names are printed on. Moreover, every American who believes president elect Joe Biden stole the 2020 election with no more facts in support of that position than the words of a US president who is on record lying to the American public over 15,413 times during his 4-year presidency according to 16th December, 2019 Washington Post. Certainly, it is highly doubtful that Caucasian America will actually police itself, or censure those in power who had a hand in emboldening this American display of lawlessness and sedition. It is to be noted that the current Acting Attorney General Jeffrey Rosen in September 2020 urged federal prosecutors to consider charging members of the Black Lives Matter movement with seditious conspiracy if they vandalized federal courthouses. Why so quiet now, Mr. Rosen? Due to 45th president Donald Trump, it certainly is the fate, of the once Great US Banana Republic Head of all Banana Republics, which by his definition is the Mother of Shithole Countries, to suffer the disdain and smirks of the entire world as he, this rogue fascist crowned US president brings the US down to the same earth it stole from Native Americans and denied to African Americans. Deal with your shame America. Everyone's watching!

MAGA: US CIVIL WAR II

In a 2006 bulletin, the FBI detailed the threat of white nationalists and skinheads infiltrating police in all 50 US States, in order to disrupt investigations against fellow members and recruit other supremacists. The killings of Afrimericans at the hands of white supremacist policemen nationwide may be attributed to the successful infiltration of US police departments, nationwide and supreme inciting by the US 45th president Donald J. Trump who repeatedly coddles white supremacists to chagrin of onlookers. He tells these racists they are loved and considered true patriots, by him. These reprobates form the base supporters of the 45th US president, and they find sympathetic words from all Americans who share similar views with the white supremacy agenda.

It is to be understood, that reality states the US is a nation of immigrants built on the backs of Afrimerican slaves, broken treaties with Native Americans, and the life-blood of veterans of every war since the First US Civil War. I say First Civil War because what the world is witness to is the spiritual rise of the South in US Civil War II. From Republican Law Makers and University professors to the average American who feels disenfranchised because he/she feels that the immigrant nation that the US is, needs to be purged of non-whites and only that will Make America Great Again (MAGA). Not everyone understands what is going on in the US, because with the current incident on Capitol Hill, many Trump supporters are claiming MAGA actually means, My Arse Got Arrested as they have been arrested by law enforcement personnel not a part of this war.

The best strategy of those in the US BLM groups, nationwide, should be a concerted effort to stay at home and refuse to be caught up in a purely Caucasian on Caucasian struggle. The crux of the matter is that the US is a nation divided not between the haves and have nots but a struggle between white supremacist Americans and white Americans whom Abraham Lincoln, and Benjamin Franklin spiritually represent. I am tired of seeing innocent Afrimericans die at the hands of US white supremacists, without the BLM placing more of people of colour in harm's way; in a struggle that doesn't concern them, at this point. Some of the groups that stormed the Capitol Building are as follows: (1) Oath keepers; (2) 3 Percenters; (3) Kraken; (4) Kakistan; (5) QAnon; (6) Volknut triangle & Thor hammer and the (7) Proud Boys. Prior to Donald J. Trump taking office, I was surprised to see myself in his presence in an astral Space. I found him to be very cordial, which was not what I expected at all. He was busy doing whatever he was focused on, and asked me a straight question the answer to which I said, "Look to the presidency of your predecessor Barack Obama". This is not the answer he wished to hear because he became visibly disturbed by my answer. Wherein I retorted, "You really despise President Obama. Don't you?" He did not have to answer. The truth was on full display for all to see. Since then, I have been able to predict Trump's behavior for the most part, so I will lay it all on the line in this short work. Donald J. Trump has no endgame. He never needed one before. He has always been able to lie his way, con his way, buy his way or bully his way out of life-situations. Trump has fallen. He put faith in the American people rallying to his aid because the US is majority Caucasian. He eschews such things as integrity, justice, compassion and the strength of such values as truth thinking the Universe really has some god somewhere in it, who actually sides with him and the entire cadre of his misogynic followers because liars, who make their living lying to millions of Americans each week fooled him into believing that their Lilly-white gods of money and influence support his cause. What's Trump's cause? The erasure of any self-empowerment Afrimericans may wield in the US. And by so doing he aims on closing the wound he received from Barack Obama, which unknown to him such a wound can never be closed. Would you see the wound? Very well. Compare Obama and Trump. Then compare their two presidencies. Using any rubric of fairness, Obama is a crowned King, while Donald has made of himself, the vilest of vile human beings. And this wound makes the 45th president of the US insane. Nancy Pelosi is wise to be fearful of Donald Trump's ability to make nuclear war or some other international destructive statement on his way out the door, because president Trump is certainly clearly insane. Trump is the twitter president. He relies on a few bites or tweets to maintain his control over his followers, who are similarly debilitated; some uneducated, prone to believe just about anything if it is heard from someone they trust, prone to lawlessness because they are Caucasians living in a country with chronic ethnohegemony; because racism, eugenics and hate of the other is systemic and a part of their institutions and culture. If President Elect Joe Biden, Nancy Pelosi, and other lawmakers do not treat their safety with the seriousness it deserves and see to their own private security but leaves that to government systems that may already be corrupted by Trump's followers, then they will become martyrs as the US becomes drenched with innocent blood. And this is the legacy of Trump. There are only three (3) reasons to remove a sitting president: For committing a crime: Should the president commit a crime, he has the same rights of due process as any other legal defendant, and therefore must be indicted of an actual crime, which involves violating a law that was passed prior to him committing the crime. The impeachment process requires agreement between both legislative bodies. The House of Representatives requires a simple majority, more than 50% of the vote, to impeach and the Senate requires a two-thirds majority. Congress impeached two presidents in US history. Congress impeached the 17th president, Andrew Johnson, after he replaced Secretary of War Edwin M. Stanton with General Ulysses S. Grant because this violated the Tenure of Office Act; and Congress impeached 42nd president Bill Jefferson Clinton on charges of perjury and obstruction of justice following Clinton's testimony about his extramarital affair during the sexual harassment lawsuit filed against him by Arkansas state employee Paula Jones. Congress neither convicted Johnson nor Clinton, and both remained in office. The second reason to remove a president from office is the Inability to Perform Presidential Duties. The third and final reason for removing a president from power is the Lack of Party or Public Popularity. Herein lies the reason that a president's party may deny supporting his/her run for a second term. There is another way to remove a president from power and that is through the use of the 25th Amendment to the Constitution which allows the president to voluntarily step aside if he feels he may be physically or emotionally unable to perform presidential duties. The amendment states that the president's cabinet may transfer the powers of the president to the vice president as determined by a majority vote. If the president challenges this decision, Congress determines whether to restore the president to power or not, but in absence of a two-thirds vote in both houses, the president returns to power. The 25th Amendment was implemented to safeguard the president who becomes unable to fulfill his duties, and works as a contingency if the president becomes incapacitated or unable to resign. Further, the provision applies if the president is captured or kidnapped and is unable to act or if concerns arise that the president is psychologically/mentally unfit to continue his term in office. On 13th January, 2021, 4th president Donald J. Trump became the only president to be impeached twice. The US House of Representatives voted to impeach president Donald J. Trump 232 'yea' to 197 'nay' with 5 'not voting' utilizing the 25th Amendment for inciting a mob of white supremacist Trump supporters to storm and takeover the Capitol Building while Trump's vice president Pence and members of the House of Representatives were inside certifying the 2020 election results and the new presidency of president elect Joe Biden and vice president elect Kamala Harris. Trump's inciting resulted in the deaths of two (2) police officers; one   female white supremacist insurrectionist and Air Force veteran Ashli Babbitt and the deaths of four other insurrectionists from other causes. Should lawmakers have impeached 45th president Donald J. Trump? Yes. Should Trump be disqualified from ever holding public office again? Certainly. Does it matter what Trump does next, as a consequence of his impeachment? No. The fact of the matter is that he is clearly insane, so shame on any Trump supporters regardless of who he or she is and what position or temporal power he/she might wield.

BLACK LIVES MATTER

Some media talking-heads, religiously minded and self-hating Afrimericans have bought into the propaganda that the US law enforcement does not have a serious problem when it comes to the murder of Afrimericans, predominantly and other racial or ethnic groups, such as Native Americans. It is my opinion, that the US has a serious problem and a large part of that problem concerns the concept of "self-identification". Afrimericans have gone from being labeled as "nigger", "negro", "Afro-American", and more recently "black". It is obvious that Afrimericans are dark-skinned, but does not make any Afrimerican "black". "Black" is a color and not a race, nor should be a part of anyone's self-identification. Through language, the 1% Super-rich uses extreme influence on the Americans. They not only control what the media reports, but manipulates everyone, Caucasian and Afrimerican alike and here's how it works. Everyone knows that Colonists enslaved Afrimericans and Native Americans, misusing both peoples in a genocidal effort to forge a new nation. To accomplish the task of enslavement, the fledgling power-structure had to supplant both the Native American and African identity, with words that would allow unconscious psychological manipulation en-masse; a trick performed on various African tribes by other African tribes who had previously adopted Islam. First, slave owners created a power vacuum within African consciousness by renaming Africans with the slaveowners surname, because one's name symbolizes his power or identity. To this, they added the derogatory appellation "nigger", "negro" and finally "black" which everyone unconsciously knows is not a race culture or ethnicity. Therefore, when every African called himself "black", he was saying to himself and the world that he is not a "person" but a "colour" meaning "thing". US slavery ended physically years ago, but because of Afrimerican ignorance on the university level on down, every African, including our President Barack Obama, the First lady and their daughters continue to deal psychologically with slavery's psychological aftermath. Dr. Maxwell Maltz, a plastic surgeon estimated that it takes twenty-one days, on average, to change one's personality and self-worth. He discovered this tidbit of information by observing hundreds of patients on whom he operated. If it takes twenty-one days to change a person's personality, what do you think is the case with Afrimericans who have endured 200 plus years of identity-destruction? Dr. Joy Degruy in her ground breaking research developed the theory of Post Traumatic Slave Syndrome based on twelve years of quantitative and qualitative research publishing her findings in her book Post Traumatic Slave Syndrome – America's Legacy of Enduring Injury and Healing". Her theory "explains the etiology of many of the adaptive survival behaviors in African American communities throughout the United States and the Diaspora. It is a condition that exists as a consequence of multigenerational oppression of Africans and their descendants resulting from centuries of chattel slavery. A form of slavery, which was predicated on the belief that African Americans were inherently/genetically inferior to whites. This was then followed by institutionalized racism, which continues to perpetuate injury". What Dr. Degruy and those interested in the survival and achievement of Afrimericans have overlooked is the smoking-gun... the single change in the entire edifice of slavery miseducation that will change each Afrimerican individual, seemingly overnight... eradication of the foreign "thing" qualification from Afrimerican psychology, returning each Afrimerican to personhood. It is for this reason I advocate Africans in the United States call themselves

Afrimericans, and henceforth and forever eliminate the idea of "black" as used to self-identify. Further, NEVER refer to Caucasians as anything but, Caucasian... these people are not "white". They never were. Notice how Republican candidate for President Trump ran on the platform, "to make America Great Again". Let us translate, candidate Trump's hidden platform by shedding a little light on both his language and behaviour. Trump has made many anti-women rights', and anti-Latin statements. Trumps platform, expressed in plain language, is not to make America great again, but to make America "White" again. In this context, he is appealing to the "white supremacist" that exists just beneath the surface of many of the majority US populace. During the Orenthal J. Simpson trial, I was extremely interested in the US polarization after the courts acquitted O. J. Simpson. Many Afrimericans saw detective Mark Fuhrman's lying under oath as a clear sign of another Afrimerican lynching, but this one was occurring on a world-stage and it wasn't just O'J. Simpson that was on trial, but in the minds of Afrimericans, it was an entire people. Every Afrimerican saw himself/herself on trial, because if the Caucasian majority could do it to O.J. Simpson, whom they lauded as such an excellent Football star, lavished goods, wealth and one of their Caucasian daughter's upon, what would they do to lesser Afrimerican mortals? This was a potential Afrimerican nightmare concealed as American Justice. On the other side, there are Caucasians, who secretly feel that Afrimericans are less intelligent than they are, and therefore must rely on 'Affirmative Action" laws to gain parity with the Caucasian majority. They perceived that an Afrimerican as murdering one of their daughters. In the Stock Photo Company, where I worked at that time, I listened to my Caucasian colleagues' expressions around the company water-cooler with great interest. On the streets of New York City, this is all everyone spoke about, privately and openly. Moreover, I observed the polarization like the arraying of the "white" and "black" chess pieces on a chessboard. Shortly, thereafter, the jury handed down the not-guilty O'J. Simpson verdict and the "white supremacists" dropped the covert façade and revealed themselves. "There is no justice in America!" As if with one accord, that is what resounded from sea to shining sea. Since then, almost every issue played out in the media, seemed to have a "white vs black" polarization, with Afrimericans claiming the injustice of a situation, and some Caucasians pointing out the "lawfulness" of some racially biased and inequitable situation. Two identical cases, the Caucasian receives community service, the Afrimerican receives 25-to-life. A law enforcement person shoots an unarmed Afrimerican child, unarmed Afrimerican man, unarmed Hispanic man, and Afrimericans cry foul, while the Caucasians claim "support law enforcement, not every situation is based on race". Of course, they are correct, race is not the basis of every situation, but the dichotomy of "white vs black", is the basis of every situation and through that language dichotomy, the 1% manipulates Caucasians, Afrimericans, and native Americans alike. Native Americans also suffer disproportionate police murders, and injustice as compared to the Caucasian population majority. According to the Lakota People's Law project report, Native Lives Matter", "Native American men are admitted to prison at four times the rate of white men and Native women at six-fold the rate of white women. Additionally, Native Americans are the racial group most likely to be killed by law enforcement". The report states that: Native American youth are found to disproportionately suffer adverse effects at the stages of arrest, diversion, detention, petition, adjudication, probation, and secure placement in the juvenile justice system. The types of unsettling reports of unfair treatment towards Native peoples by law enforcement are not isolated incidents—rather they are endemic of a justice system, which discriminates against the Native American population. On a given day, 1 in 25 American Indians age 18 or older is under the jurisdiction of the criminal justice system. Unconscionable examples set by state leaders have become a model for state employees to follow. The roots of these problems lay within the nexus of money and racism. Local organizing must continue in our community. If Rapid City and the rest of South Dakota are to understand our position, we must speak in unison, explicitly to these issues. Although Native youth are only 1 percent of the national youth population, 70 percent of youth committed to the Federal Bureau of Prisons (BOP) as delinquents are Native American, as are 31 percent of youth committed to the BOP as adults. In 26 states, Native youth are disproportionately placed in secure confinement in comparison to their population. In South Dakota, Alaska, North Dakota, and Montana, Native youth account for 29% - 42% of youth in secure confinement. Of 32% youth Nationwide, placed in secure facilities, 74% are Native American. From 2004 - 2008, there was a 92% tribal youth conviction rate and 87% non-tribal youth conviction rate. The Guardian Newspaper, conducted a 2015 study on law enforcement killings in the US, and this is what their research uncovered: In 2015, Police were 9 times more likely to kill young African Americans than Caucasian males. In 2015, law enforcement was responsible for 1,134 deaths and despite making up only 2% of the total US population, African American males between the ages of 15 - 34 comprised more than 15% of these deaths. African American males' deaths were five times higher than that for white men of the same age. Police are responsible for one in every 65 young African American deaths. In 2015, black people were killed at twice the rate of white, Hispanic and Native Americans. African Americans were twice as likely to be unarmed when killed. "This epidemic is disproportionately affecting black people," said Brittany Packnett, an activist and member of the White House taskforce on policing. "We are wasting so many promising young lives by continuing to allow this to happen." Further, Packnett said, "The criminal justice system is presenting no deterrent to the excessive use of deadly force by police. On 12th May, 2015, Samuel V. Jones wrote an article entitled, "Elephant in the Living Room: White Supremacists w/ Badges & Guns murdering black men", for the Grio, an Afrimerican News site. I quote, "Because of intensifying civil strife over the recent killings of unarmed black men and boys, many Americans are wondering, "What's wrong with our police?" Remarkably, one of the most compelling but unexplored explanations may rest with a FBI warning of October 2006, which reported that "White supremacist infiltration of law enforcement" represented a significant national threat. Several key events preceded the report. A federal court found that members of a Los Angeles sheriff's department formed a Neo Nazi gang and habitually terrorized the black community. Later, the Chicago police department fired Jon Burge, a detective with reputed ties to the Ku Klux Klan, after discovering he tortured over 100 black male suspects. Thereafter, the Mayor of Cleveland discovered that many of the city police locker rooms were infested with "White Power" graffiti. Years later, a Texas sheriff department discovered that two of its deputies were recruiters for the Klan. In near prophetic fashion, after the FBI's warning, white supremacy extremism in the U.S. increased, exponentially. From 2008 to 2014, the number of white supremacist groups, reportedly, grew from 149 to nearly a 1,000, with no apparent abatement in their infiltration of law enforcement. This year, alone, at least seven San Francisco law enforcement officers were suspended after an investigation revealed they exchanged numerous "White Power" communications laden with remarks about "lynching African-Americans and burning crosses." Three (3) reputed Klan members that served as correction officers were arrested for conspiring to murder a black inmate. At least four (4) Fort Lauderdale police officers were fired after an investigation found that the officers fantasized about killing black suspects". The United States doesn't publicly track white supremacists, so the full range of their objectives remains murky": Although black and Jewish-Americans are believed to be the foremost targets of white supremacists, Recent attacks in Nevada, Wisconsin, Arizona, Kansas and North Carolina, demonstrate that other non-whites, and religious and social minorities, are also vulnerable. Perhaps more alarmingly, in the last several years alone, white supremacists have reportedly murdered law enforcement officers in Arkansas, Nevada and Wisconsin. The FBI reports that of the 511 law enforcement officers killed during felony incidents from 2004 to 2013, white citizens killed the majority of them. Of the citizens stopped by law enforcement officers in New York City and Chicago, white citizens were more likely to be found with guns and drugs. Given the white supremacist penchant for violence, guns and drug trafficking, the findings may be an indication that their network is just as destructive and far-reaching as that of foreign terrorist groups. "The unfortunate consequence of today's threat is that a law enforcement officer may be good or bad, a villain or hero; one exceptionally prone to exhibit malicious forms of racial hatred, or distinctively suited to protect the racially oppressed. But the paradox doesn't end there. The white supremacist threat brings to light a dark feature of the American experience that some believed extinct. It rouses ingrained notions of distrusts between police and communities of color while bringing to bear the vital interest citizens of goodwill share in the complete abolishment of race as a judgmental factor. As the nation struggles to resolve the perplexities of police brutality, the white supremacist threat should inform all Americans that today's civil discord is not borne out of a robust animosity towards law enforcement, most of whom are professional. Rather, it's more representative of a centuries-old ideological clash, which has ignited in citizens of goodwill a desire to affirm notions of racial equality so that the moral ethos of American culture is a reality for all". A Guardian investigation took a detailed look at extensive flaws in the FBI's Fatal Police Shootings Database. Federal law requires that police departments nationwide, report police involved killings. The Guardian researched the FBI's Database on police involved killings for the period 2004 – 2014 and discovered that the FBI's database is woefully inadequate. According to the Guardian's research: In 2014, only 244, which is 1.2 percent of the nation's 18,000 law enforcement agencies reported fatal police shootings. Respective police agencies did not report Eric Garner's death in New York, Tamir Rice and John Crawford's deaths in Ohio. The NYPD submitted data for only one year, 2006, across the investigated period, but even the NYPD's year 2006 data did not match the FBI's NYC 2006 death count. The FBI has 32 circumstance reporting categories. One category collects "Felon killed by police", and none collects "Unarmed Civilian Killed by Police". Some police departments Lied on their submitted data claiming "Police

Unjustified Civilian Killings As 'Civilian Killings Of Civilians'. The police charged and/or convicted murders of civilians Oscar Grant, Rekia Boyd, Malissa Williams, and Timothy Russell were not even in the FBI's database at all. The rising tide of Police shootings corresponded with a rise in agencies reporting their figures so The Guardian was unable to discern and decade long trends. White Supremacists cold-bloodedly murdered Texas' Kaufman County Assistant District Attorney, Mark Hasse and several months later, District Attorney Mike McLelland and his wife. A 2006, FBI report entitled, "White Supremacist Infiltration of Law Enforcement", states that the threat they pose is due to unrestricted access they possess to sabotage and circumvent law enforcement processes, and access to elected officials and protected persons whom they perceive as targets for violence. The intelligence gathered by the infiltration of just one white supremacist group can benefit other white supremacist groups because of the multiple allegiances' groups hold. The areas of infiltration can lead to investigative breaches, which would jeopardize the lives of law enforcement sources, personnel and 'minorities. In 2004, the term "ghost skins" came to the FBI's attention. It refers to white supremacists who avoid overt displays of their white supremacist beliefs, while adopting a role-playing façade that allows them to covertly blend into society and promote white supremacist causes. Moreover, the FBI reports that there are law enforcement officials whose support for white supremacist causes are under FBI investigation. However, who these officials are, and how extensive the FBI investigation into these officials is a matter for speculation, since that information was removed before the FBI made the report public. We should realize that United States issues are not "black vs white" ones, but the ongoing struggle of Native Americans,

Afrimericans and other ethnicities to establish self-identity and sovereignty in a sea of distractions where a small group wields greater and greater financial power to the detriment of all. Therefore, we may conclude that in the nationwide law enforcement infiltration of some fraction of 18,000 police departments, lies the source of every law enforcement murder of unarmed civilians nationwide, over a 12-year period, beginning in 2004 and increasing exponentially into 2016; as well as the source of the corruption of Caucasian judges, juries, and prosecutors.

CHAPTER TWO

PRECEDENCE FOR SLAVERY

Since 2019, the world has been under a coronavirus biological attack by the creation of Covid-19 virus. From an African perspective, this is just another salvo in the ongoing ethnohegemonic struggle between the world's elite and the rest of the planet. Past history justifies this perspective, so there is no hint of conspiracy theory or any other denigrating depiction associated with this viewpoint. Let's take cognizance of a few historical highlights…

"Assortments of diseased, damaged, and disabled Negroes, deemed incurable and otherwise worthless, are bought up, it seems, (cheap, no doubt, like old iron,) by medical institutions, to be experimented and operated upon, for purposes of "medical education"

and the interests of "medical science!" Moreover, J. Marion Sims (1845 – 1849) the US "father of gynecology," performed medical experiments on enslaved African women without anesthesia causing their deaths from infection after his surgeries. Advertisements such as this one in the Charleston S. C. Mercury, Oct.12, 1838, advertisement, by Dr. T. Stillman, on behalf of the "Medical Infirmary," is typical: "To Planters and Others—Wanted, fifty Negroes. Any person, having sick Negroes, considered incurable by their respective physicians, and wishing to dispose of them, Dr. S. will pay cash for Negroes affected with scrofula, or king's evil, confirmed hypochondriacs, apoplexy, diseases of the liver, kidneys, spleen, stomach and intestines, bladder and its appendages, diarrhea, dysentery, etc. The highest cash price will be paid, on application as above," (viz., Medical Infirmary, No. 110 Church street, Charleston)" (American Slave Code pg. 86 -87). George C. Wilson March 9, 1977 (Washington Post) wrote that the Army disclosed that it secretly conducted 239 germ warfare tests in open air between 1949 and 1969, some tests releasing live but supposedly harmless microscope "bugs" at Washington's Greyhound bus terminal and National Airport as part of the experiment. The idea, according to a two-volume report the Army gave to the senate health subcommittee yesterday, was to learn how to wage biological warfare and defend against it. The Washington tests started in 1949 at an undisclosed location and were conducted again in May, 1965, at the bus terminal and airport. Washington was one of five cities where the Army released simulated lethal germs i public places. Other cities where the public served as unknowing guinea pigs were New York, San Francisco, Key West and Panama City, Fla.A11 told, the Army listed 27 times that it tested simulated toxins on public property, including releasing spores in two tunnels on a stretch of Pennsylvania Turnpike. In addition to those experiments in public places, the

Army secretary used military personnel and their families for open air experiments by spraying simulated germs into the air at a number of bases, including Fort Detrick, Md.; Fort Belvoir, Va.; and the Marine training school at Quantico, Va. The Army said in its report that the tests were "essential" to "substantiate theories and fill knowledge gaps and to determine vulnerability to attack." The live bacteria the Army employed were deemed harmless at the time, the report said. But Sen. Richard S. Scheweiker (R-Pa.) told Army witnesses at the Senate subcommittee hearing yesterday that "it is very risky indeed to assume that any living organism, reduced to germ warfare size and released in a populated area, is ever safe." In the 1950 San Francisco tests, the bacteria Seriatta Marcescens were used. Medical searchers suspect it may have caused 11 cases pneumonia in the bay area. The Army said three laboratory scientists at Fort Detrick died from diseases contracted in the 1950s and 1960s, as had been reported previously. Another 504 workers connected with biological warfare activities at Ft. Detrick, Dugway proving Ground and the Deseret test Center in Utah and the Pine Bluff Arsenal in Arkansas suffered infections, according to the Army's count. The Army released its censored report, believed the most complete official version of this nation's biological warfare effort, as Chairman Edward M. Kennedy (D-Mass.) of the Senate health subcommittee convened a hearing on the subject. Kennedy released a summary of a separate Central Intelligence Agency report which showed that the Office of Strategic Services, predecessor of the CIA used germ warfare against the head of Nazi Germany's Reichsbank during World War 11 to prevent him from attending an economic meeting. IN what is believed the first official acknowledgement that the United States engaged in germ warfare, OSS agents managed to give Hjalmar Schact, Nazi

Germany's leading banker, food poisoning. The CIA summary did not supply the date or how the poison was administered. The Army, in its two-volume report, traced the history of the U.S. biological warfare program from 1942 when President Nixon renounced the use of biology weapons. The military's effort since then, according to the Army, had been confined to studying defensive measures against biology warfare. The Army report said testing of biological warfare agents rose sharply after May, 1961 when then Defense Secretary Robert S. McNamara ordered the Joint Chiefs of Staff to "evaluate the potentialities" of both biological and chemical warfare, "considering all possible applications. "The Joint Chiefs, the report said estimated it would cost $4 billion to obtain "McNamara's complete spectrum" of biological and chemical warfare capability. The Pentagon's research the director at the time, Harold Brown, who is now Secretary of Defense, "strongly concurred in the JCS view that these weapons had great potential," according to the report which mentioned Brown by position but not by name. McNamara accepted the Joint Chief's recommendations as modified by Brown's office, the report said, and a detailed chemical and biological warfare program was laid down. "Overall," the report continued. "The project resulted in large increases in U.S. Army BW [biology warfare] programs." in releasing the two-volume report, Army Secretary Clifford L. Alexander said that the Army's biological warfare program from its inception was characterized by continuing in depth review and participation by the most eminent scientists, medical consultants, industrial experts and government officials." Brig. Gen. William S. Augerson, Army assistant surgeon general, told the senate subcommittee that the Army sometimes used human volunteers for biological experiments but projected them to a degree which "equaled or exceeded" civilian safeguards. "We know of no death of permanent injury in any volunteer in this program," Augerson said. On 29th October 2018, the Agence de Presse Africaine reported: "Odinga said girls and women between 14 and 49 from the fastest growing populations in the country will not have children, because of a state-sponsored sterilization exercise that was sold to the country as a tetanus vaccination. The Catholic Church was ignored when it mounted a strong but lonely campaign against the mass tetanus vaccination, after it raised concerns about the safety of the vaccine that was being used, he said. At the time, the Catholic Church in Kenya claimed that the tetanus vaccine used by the government of Kenya and UN agencies was contaminated with a hormone (BhCG) that can cause miscarriages and render some women sterile. "The Church's position was informed by what had happened in Mexico, Nicaragua and Philippines, where the various governments together with WHO/UNICEF had conducted similar campaigns using tetanus toxoid impregnated with beta human chorionic gonadotropin (BhCG) that causes permanent infertility among girls and women," Odinga continued. Odinga says they confirmed through analysis of samples that the vaccines used were tainted with the hormone. "Today, we can confirm to the country that the Catholic Church was right. Hundreds of thousands of our girls and women, aged between 14 and 49, from the fastest growing populations in the country will not have children, because of the state-sponsored sterilization that was sold to the country as tetanus vaccination," he declared. After Agriq-Quest's license was suspended, the company pointed the finger at the government. They claimed that the government's decision to suspend their license was due to the fact that Agriq-Quest refused to doctor the tests for them. According to Business Daily Africa, when Agriq-Quest conducted the tests on the vaccines, they found the Catholic Church's suspicions to be correct. As BDA reported, "The company's results from tests carried out on the vials showed that the samples of the vaccines were contaminated as had been claimed by the Catholic Church and Agriq-Quest claimed the government wanted the results altered to show that they were fit to be administered to women and children." According to Odinga, as reported by APA, the government, for some mysterious reason, was hell-bent on misleading the country, while intentionally sterilizing Kenyan girls and women. "The vaccines were a great crime committed against women. Women should choose when to have children and how to space them," he said. It is important to point out that the belief that tetanus vaccinations sterilizing citizens has been a long-time controversy in Kenya and has been disproven prior to these claims. Also, after the discussion came to a head, in spite of claims of tests showing contamination, UNICEF and the World Health Organization later said that the vaccines were safe and procured from a pre-qualified manufacturer. However, according to Odinga, they accessed the analysis from four highly regarded institutions, such as Agriq Quest Ltd, the Nairobi Hospital Laboratories, the University of Nairobi and Lancet Kenya. "These results all indicate that the Tetanus Toxoid Vaccine had high contents of beta human chorionic gonadotropin hormone (BhCG) that causes sterility in women." According to Kenya's opposition leader, Raila Odinga, half-a-million young girls are now infertile following a tetanus vaccine administered by the government in 2014 and 2015. The controversy played on for several years, but came to a head in 2016 when Agriq-Quest Ltd, a Nairobi-based pharmaceutical company disputed with Kenya's Ministry of Health over the tetanus and polio vaccinations. Catholic doctors made accusations claiming the vaccines contained a hormone dangerous to young women that causes sterilization, but WHO, UNICEF and the Kenyan Health Ministry maintained the charges were false and the vaccine safe. As we see, now ½ million Kenyan women became infertile because of the vaccines that is a Frankenstein lie.

THE LAW OF DISCOVERY

The non-European world was colonized under a Colonial international legal principle known today as the Doctrine of Discovery. This Doctrine authorized European, Christian countries to explore and claim the lands and rights of non-Europeans. Robert J. Miller -—Professor Lewis & Clark Law School, Portland, Oregon; Chief Justice, Confederated Tribes of the Grand Ronde Community of Oregon; Citizen, Eastern Shawnee Tribe of Oklahoma; Board of Directors, Tribal Leadership Forum and Oregon Historical Society. -—In his paper "The International Law of Colonialism: A Comparative Analysis", states: The majority of the non-European world was colonized under an international legal principle that is known today as the Doctrine of Discovery. The Doctrine is one of the very first international law principles and allegedly authorized European, Christian countries to explore and claim the lands and rights of peoples outside of Europe. When European countries set out to exploit new lands in the fifteenth through twentieth centuries, and planted their flags and crosses in ——newly discovered lands, they were undertaking the well-recognized procedures and rituals of Discovery to make claims to these territories and over Indigenous peoples. In fact, the Doctrine provided that Europeans automatically acquired property rights in native lands and gained governmental, political, and commercial rights over the Indigenous inhabitants without their knowledge or consent. This legal principle was created and justified by religious, racial, and ethnocentric ideas of European and Christian superiority over other peoples and religions. The Doctrine is still international and domestic law today and is being actively applied against Indigenous peoples and nations. For example, American, Canadian, New Zealand, Australian, and international courts have struggled with questions regarding Discovery and Indigenous land titles in recent decades. And in 2007 and 2010, Russia and China evoked the Doctrine by planting their flags on the Arctic Ocean and South China Sea beds to claim commercial and sovereign rights. Professor Peter d'Errico, Native Americans in America: A Theoretical and Historical Overview, in, American Nations: Encounters in Indian Country 1850 to the present said: Detailed reassessment of early history may seem unnecessary to a present understanding of Native Americans. Some may think it enough to acknowledge the fallaciousness of the notion of ——discovery, with all it implies in the way of colonial arrogance. But the fact that ——discovery became part of the institutional structure of America means that America consists of a continual reaffirmation of colonialism. The nature of this colonialism explains much of the present scene. According to Robert J. Miller, the 1823 United States Supreme Court decision of Johnson v. McIntosh held the Doctrine of Discovery as a European and American established colonial law as well as an American federal and state government law. Discovering countries automatically gained sovereign and property rights in the lands they discovered even though indigenous people were already occupying them. The real property right Europeans acquired, was an exclusive future right, a title held by the discovering

European country in the lands, subject to the continuing use and occupancy rights of the Indigenous peoples. Discovering countries gained sovereign governmental powers over the native peoples and their governments, restricting tribal international political, commercial, and diplomatic powers. Discovery gives exclusive title to discovering countries, therefore indigenous land owners' rights to complete sovereignty, as independent nations, are curtailed, and their power to dispose of the soil at their own will, to whomsoever they pleased, is denied. Indigenous nations are pre-empted from selling their lands to anyone except the discovering European country because the discovering country acquired an exclusive option to buy tribal lands whenever tribal governments consented to sell. The 'Terra Nullius' principle applied, meaning it does not matter whether the land is occupied or unoccupied, used or unused, the discovering European country had legal rights to it since non-Christians do not have the same rights as Christians, whom the Christian god had chosen to rule over non-Christians. A European country's first discovery granted property and sovereign rights over the lands its Indigenous owners. This became a bona fide title, only after the discovering country permanently occupied and possessed the discovered lands. The occupying country gained the 'pre-emption' property right, which is the sole right to usurp the land from the Indigenous peoples through attrition. The law considered that due to the primacy of 'Might is Right', indigenous people immediately lost title to their lands once occupied and could only sell it to the occupiers. The Indigenous peoples could only interact with the occupying country. The occupying country possessed a legal claim to land contiguous to their actual discoveries and settlements so that the discovery of a river mouth created a claim over all the lands drained by that river, no matter how far the distance. The Doctrine of Discovery, judges' people by alien standards not designed for them, makes no allowance for their inability to understand it, and takes no account of conditions which should except them from its exactions; measuring the people and cultures thousands of years older than the savagery of colonialism by the myopic cultural maxims of the supremacy falsehood, which is nothing more than the savagery of the bully; might over right, the foundation of European immorality and the strongest prejudices of the Caucasian nature. It seeks, by argument and inference only, to extend over non-Christians; over the Indigenous members of global communities separated by race, by tradition, by the universally given freedom of an unencumbered life, the alien, the colonial 'might is right ideology' that seeks to impose upon all the beliefs of Caucasian civility, that unknown code, and to subject them to the forced responsibilities of rules and penalties of foreigners. It tries non-Christians not by their peers, nor by the customs of their people, nor the law of their land, but by the alien customs of a different race, according to the rules of aliens, opposed to the traditions of their history, to the habits of their lives, finds all Indigenous people and non-Christians guilty a priori, then executing those races, ethnicities, and cultures. Without doubt, without equivocation or mental reservation, the Doctrine of Discovery, law of supremacy, is the most despicable legal principle a humanoid could conceive. Moreover, it brands its creators for all time as humanoids, separate and distinct from all the peoples it seeks to dominate, rule and exterminate, since no human could ever devise such an inhumane principle. And no human ever did.

WHITE SUPREMACISTS EXPERIMENT ON HUMANS

"Assortments of diseased, damaged, and disabled Negroes, deemed incurable and otherwise worthless, are bought up, it seems, (cheap, no doubt, like old iron,) by medical institutions, to be experimented and operated upon, for purposes of "medical education"

and the interests of "medical science!" Moreover, J. Marion Sims (1845 – 1849) the US "father of gynecology," performed medical experiments on enslaved African women without anesthesia causing their deaths from infection after his surgeries. Advertisements

such as tis one in the Charleston S. C. Mercury, Oct.12, 1838, advertisement, by Dr. T. Stillman, on behalf of the "Medical Infirmary," is typical: "To Planters and Others—Wanted, fifty Negroes. Any person, having sick Negroes, considered incurable by their respective physicians, and wishing to dispose of them, Dr. S. will pay cash for Negroes affected with scrofula, or king's evil, confirmed hypochondriacs, apoplexy, diseases of the liver, kidneys, spleen, stomach and intestines, bladder and its appendages, diarrhea,

dysentery, etc. The highest cash price will be paid, on application as above," (viz., Medical Infirmary, No. 110 Church street, Charleston)" (American Slave Code pg. 86 -87). George C. Wilson March 9, 1977 (Washington Post) wrote that the Army disclosed that it secretly conducted 239 germ warfare tests in open air between 1949 and 1969, some tests releasing live but supposedly harmless microscope "bugs" at Washington's Greyhound bus terminal and National Airport as part of the experiment. The idea, according to a two-volume report the Army gave to the senate health subcommittee yesterday, was to learn how to wage biological warfare and defend against it. The Washington tests started in 1949 at an undisclosed location and were conducted again in May, 1965, at the bus terminal and airport. Washington was one of five cities where the Army released simulated lethal germs i public places. Other cities where the public served as unknowing guinea pigs were New York, San Francisco, Key West and Panama City, Fla.A11 told, the Army listed 27 times that it tested simulated toxins on public property, including releasing spores in two tunnels on a stretch of Pennsylvania Turnpike. In addition to those experiments in public places, the Army secretary used military personnel and their families for open air experiments by spraying simulated germs into the air at a number of bases, including Fort Detrick, Md.; Fort Belvoir, Va.; and the Marine training school at Quantico, Va. The Army said in its report that the tests were "essential" to "substantiate theories and fill knowledge gaps and to determine vulnerability to attack." The live bacteria the Army employed were deemed harmless at the time, the report said. But Sen. Richard S. Scheweiker (R-Pa.) told Army witnesses at the Senate subcommittee hearing yesterday that "it is very risky indeed to assume that any living organism, reduced to germ warfare size and released in a populated area, is ever safe." In the 1950 San Francisco tests, the bacteria Seriatta Marcescens were used. Medical searchers suspect it may have caused 11 cases pneumonia in the bay area. The Army said three laboratory scientists at Fort Detrick died from diseases contracted in the 1950s and 1960s, as had been reported previously. Another 504 workers connected with biological warfare activities at Ft. Detrick, Dugway proving Ground and the Deseret test Center in Utah and the Pine Bluff Arsenal in Arkansas suffered infections, according to the Army's count. The Army released its censored report, believed the most complete official version of this nation's biological warfare effort, as Chairman Edward M. Kennedy (D-Mass.) of the Senate health subcommittee convened a hearing on the subject. Kennedy released a summary of a separate Central Intelligence Agency report which showed that the Office of Strategic Services, predecessor of the CIA used germ warfare against the head of Nazi Germany's Reichsbank during World War 11 to prevent him from attending an economic meeting. IN what is believed the first official acknowledgement that the United States engaged in germ warfare, OSS agents managed to give Hjalmar Schact, Nazi Germany's leading banker, food poisoning. The CIA summary did not supply the date or how the poison was administered. The Army, in its two-volume report, traced the history of the U.S. biological warfare program from 1942 when President Nixon renounced the use of biology weapons. The military's effort since then, according to the Army, had been confined to studying defensive measures against biology warfare. The Army report said testing of biological warfare agents rose sharply after May, 1961 when then Defense Secretary Robert S. McNamara ordered the Joint Chiefs of Staff to "evaluate the potentialities" of both biological and chemical warfare, "considering all possible applications. "The Joint Chiefs, the report said estimated it would cost $4 billion to obtain "McNamara's complete spectrum" of biological and chemical warfare capability. The Pentagon's research the director at the time, Harold Brown, who is now Secretary of Defense, "strongly concurred in the JCS view that these weapons had great potential," according to the report which mentioned Brown by position but not by name. McNamara accepted the Joint Chief's recommendations as modified by Brown's office, the report said, and a detailed chemical and biological warfare program was laid down. "Overall," the report continued. "The project resulted in large increases in U.S. Army BW [biology warfare] programs." in releasing the two-volume report, Army Secretary Clifford L. Alexander said that the Army's biological warfare program from its inception was characterized by continuing in depth review and participation by the most eminent scientists, medical consultants, industrial experts and government officials." Brig. Gen. William S. Augerson, Army assistant surgeon general, told the senate subcommittee that the Army sometimes used human volunteers for biological experiments but projected them to a degree which "equaled or exceeded" civilian safeguards. "We know of no death of permanent injury in any volunteer in this program," Augerson said. On 29th October 2018, the Agence de Presse Africaine reported: "Odinga said girls and women between 14 and 49 from the fastest growing populations in the country will not have children, because of a state-sponsored sterilization exercise that was sold to the country as a tetanus vaccination. The Catholic Church was ignored when it mounted a strong but lonely campaign against the mass tetanus vaccination, after it raised concerns about the safety of the vaccine that was being used, he said. At the time, the Catholic Church in Kenya claimed that the tetanus vaccine used by the government of Kenya and UN agencies was contaminated with a hormone (BhCG) that can cause miscarriages and render some women sterile. "The Church's position was informed by what had happened in Mexico, Nicaragua and Philippines, where the various governments together with WHO/UNICEF had conducted similar campaigns using tetanus toxoid impregnated with beta human chorionic gonadotropin (BhCG) that causes permanent infertility among girls and women," Odinga continued. Odinga says they confirmed through analysis of samples that the vaccines used were tainted with the hormone. "Today, we can confirm to the country that the Catholic Church was right. Hundreds of thousands of our girls and women, aged between 14 and 49, from the fastest growing populations in the country will not have children, because of the state-sponsored sterilization that was sold to the country as tetanus vaccination," he declared. After Agriq-Quest's license was suspended, the company pointed the finger at the government. They claimed that the government's decision to suspend their license was due to the fact that Agriq-Quest refused to doctor the tests for them. According to Business Daily Africa, when Agriq-Quest conducted the tests on the vaccines, they found the Catholic Church's suspicions to be correct. As BDA reported, "The company's results from tests carried out on the vials showed that the samples of the vaccines were contaminated as had been claimed by the Catholic Church and Agriq-Quest claimed the government wanted the results altered to show that they were fit to be administered to women and children." According to Odinga, as reported by APA, the government, for some mysterious reason, was hell-bent on misleading the country, while intentionally sterilizing Kenyan girls and women. "The vaccines were a great crime committed against women. Women should choose when to have children and how to space them," he said. It is important to point out that the belief that tetanus vaccinations sterilizing citizens has been a long-time controversy in Kenya and has been disproven prior to these claims. Also, after the discussion came to a head, in spite of claims of tests showing contamination, UNICEF and the World Health Organization later said that the vaccines were safe and procured from a pre-qualified manufacturer. However, according to Odinga, they accessed the analysis from four highly regarded institutions, such as Agriq Quest Ltd, the Nairobi Hospital Laboratories, the University of Nairobi and Lancet Kenya. "These results all indicate that the Tetanus Toxoid Vaccine had high contents of beta human chorionic gonadotropin hormone (BhCG) that causes sterility in women." According to Kenya's opposition leader, Raila Odinga, half-a-million young girls are now infertile following a tetanus vaccine administered by the government in 2014 and 2015. The controversy played on for several years, but came to a head in 2016 when Agriq-Quest Ltd, a Nairobi-based pharmaceutical company disputed with Kenya's Ministry of Health over the tetanus and polio vaccinations. Catholic doctors made accusations claiming the vaccines contained a hormone dangerous to young women that causes sterilization, but WHO, UNICEF and the Kenyan Health Ministry maintained the charges were false and the vaccine safe. As we see, now ½ million Kenyan women became infertile because of the vaccines that is a Frankenstinian lie.

WHY AMERICANS UPHOLD WHITE SUPREMACY

Eleven Southern states seceded from the union of the United States of America, with Missouri and Kentucky secession supporters declaring secession, but their pro-union legislatures disavowing it. These eleven rebel states formed the "Confederate States of America" (CSA): South Carolina 12/20/1860; Mississippi 01/09/1861; Florida 01/10/1861; Alabama 01/11/1861; Georgia 01/19/1861); Louisiana 01/26/1861; Texas 02/01/1861; Virginia 04/17/1861; Arkansas 05/06/1861; North Carolina 05/20/1861; and Tennessee 06/08/1861. In its declaration of secession, South Carolina wrote: "An ordinance to dissolve the Union between the State of South

Carolina and other States united with her, under the compact entitled the Constitution, of the United States of America. We, the People of the State of South Carolina, in Convention assembled, do declare and ordain, and it is hereby declared and ordained, that the ordinance adopted by us in Convention on the 23rd day of May, in the year of our Lord 1788, whereby the Constitution of the United States was ratified, and also all acts and parts of acts of the general assembly of this State, ratifying the amendments of the said Constitution, are hereby repealed, and that the Union now subsisting between South Carolina and other States, under the name of the United States of America, is dissolved." Now, the reason these eleven CSA considered themselves and were considered rebel states is because the secession of these states from the union of the United Sates into a confederacy of states was a breaking of each of their oaths in their ratification of the US Constitution and therefore each of them stood in violation of that overriding constitutional law. In 1788, the people of South Carolina adopted the US Constitution and relinquished all legal right to reject it as the governing and "Supreme law of the land". South Carolina ratified the US Constitution with the following words: "The Convention, having maturely considered the Constitution, or form of government, reported to Congress by the convention of delegates from the United States of America, and submitted to them, by a resolution of the Legislature of this State passed the 17th and 18th days of February last, in order to form a more perfect Union, establish justice, ensure domestic tranquility, provide for the common defense, promote the general welfare, and secure the blessings of liberty to the people of the said United States and their posterity, do, in the name and in behalf of the people of this State, hereby assent to and ratify the same." Moreover, what applies to South Carolina applies to all states that ratified the US Constitution since the act of ratification is not an ordinance, nor was it called an ordinance; therefore, ratification cannot be legally repealed by any subsequent ordnance: "This Constitution and the Laws of the United States made in pursuance thereof, and the treaties made or which shall be made under the authority of the United States, shall be the supreme law of the land, and the judges in every State shall be bound thereby, anything in the Constitution or laws of any State to the contrary notwithstanding." Further, the constitution expressly prohibits states as follows: " No State shall enter into any treaty, alliance, or confederation, grant letters of marque or reprisal: no State shall, without the consent of Congress, lay any duty of tonnage, keep troops or ships of war in time of peace, enter into any agreement or compact with another State, or with a foreign power, or engage in war, unless actually invaded, or in such imminent danger as will not admit of delay." On Dec. 24, 1860, delegates at South Carolina's secession convention adopted a "Declaration of the Immediate Causes Which Induce and Justify the Secession of South Carolina from the Federal Union." It noted "an increasing hostility on the part of the non-slaveholding States to the institution of slavery", protesting that Northern states had failed to "fulfill their constitutional obligations" by interfering with the return of fugitive slaves to bondage. Further, New York no longer allowed slavers to have slaves accompany them when entering New York, and African men could vote in New England states, as well as openly advocate for slavery's end. Mississippi's secession declaration stated: "Our position is thoroughly identified with the institution of slavery, the greatest material interest of the world. Its labor supplies the product which constitutes by far the largest and most important portions of the commerce of the earth. These products are peculiar to the climate verging the tropical regions, and by an imperious law of nature none but the black race can bear exposure to the tropical sun. These products have become necessities of the world, and a blow to slavery is a blow at commerce and civilization." Secession Commissioner S.F. Hale of Alabama urged Kentucky to secede to avoid racial equality and the "lust of half-civilized Africans." Hale said: "At the time of the adoption of the Federal Constitution, African slavery existed in twelve of the thirteen States. Slaves are recognized both as property, and as a basis of political power, by the Federal Compact, and special provisions are made by that instrument for their protection as property. Under the influences of climate, and other causes, slavery has been banished from the Northern States, the slaves themselves have been sent to the Southern States, and there sold, and their price gone into the pockets of their former owners at the North. And in the meantime, African Slavery has not only become one of the fixed domestic institutions of the Southern States, but forms an important element of their political power, and constitutes the most valuable species of their property—worth, according to recent estimates, not less than $4,000,000,000.00; forming, in fact, the basis upon which rests the prosperity and wealth of most of these States, and supplying the commerce of the world with its richest freights, and furnishing the manufactories of two continents with the raw material, and their operatives with bread. It is upon this gigantic interest, this peculiar institution of the South, that the Northern States and their people have been waging an unrelenting and fanatical war for the last quarter of a century. An institution with which is bound up, not only the wealth and prosperity of the Southern people, but their very existence as a political community. At the Florida Secession

Convention, John C. Pelot, of Alachua county, made the case for Florida's secession: "Why all this? The story is soon told. In the formation of the Government of our Fathers, the Constitution of 1787, the institution of domestic slavery is recognized, and the right of property in slaves is expressly guaranteed. The People of a portion of the States who were parties to the Government were early opposed to the institution. The feeling of opposition to it has been cherished, and fostered, and inflamed until it has taken possession of the public mind of the North to such an extent that it overwhelms every other influence. It has seized the political power and now threatens annihilation to slavery throughout the Union. At the South, and with our People of course, slavery is the element of all value, and a destruction of that destroys all that is property. This party, now soon to take possession of the powers of the Government, is sectional, irresponsible to us, and driven on by an infuriated fanatical madness that defies all opposition, must inevitably destroy every vestige or right growing out of property in slaves. Gentlemen, the State of Florida is now a member of the Union under the power of the Government, so to go into the hands of this party. As we stand our doom is decreed." The Texas case for secession read: In all the non-slave-holding States, in violation of that good faith and comity which should exist between entirely distinct nations, the people have formed themselves into a great sectional party, now strong enough in numbers to control the affairs of each of those States, based upon the unnatural feeling of hostility to these Southern States and their beneficent and patriarchal system of African slavery, proclaiming the debasing doctrine of the equality of all men, irrespective of race or color—a doctrine at war with nature, in opposition to the experience of mankind, and in violation of the plainest revelations of the Divine

Law. They demand the abolition of negro slavery throughout the confederacy, the recognition of political equality between the white and the negro races, and avow their determination to press on their crusade against us, so long as a negro slave remains in these States. Louisiana Commissioner George Williamson urged Texas to secede "to preserve the blessings of African slavery": Louisiana supplies to Texas a market for her surplus wheat, grain and stock; both States have large areas of fertile, uncultivated lands, peculiarly adapted to slave labor; and they are both so deeply interested in African slavery that it may be said to be necessary to their existence, and is the keystone to the arch of their prosperity... The people of the slave holding States are bound together by the same necessity and determination to preserve African slavery... That constitution of the Southern States has never violated, and taking it as the basis of our new government we hope to form a slave-holding confederacy that will secure to us and our remotest posterity the great blessings its authors designed in the Federal Union. With the social balance wheel of slavery to regulate its machinery, we may fondly indulge the hope that our Southern government will be perpetual.

ROMAN CIVIL LAW

Senator Elizabeth Warren famously said "If you don't have a seat at the table, you're probably on the menu", and in reference to Afrimericans living in the United States of America her statement is prophetic as long as white supremacy exists within a single American heart. The United States harbors many slavery apologists. Yet, that is because the US education whitewashes, covers and misconstrues the fact concerning this most despicable of institutions. We will endeavor to uncover the institutions true face through its laws, precepts and first-hand ex-slave testimonies. From the outset, it is to be noted that States professed that pre-Christian "Roman Civil Law" contains the principles of their "peculiar institution" namely African Enslavement. US Colonial Laws/Statutes regarding slaveholders' humane treatment of slaves were worthless, not worth the paper on which they are written, because no Caucasian was ever prosecuted for murdering slaves. Since, "The master is not liable to an indictment for a battery committed upon his slave" (Wheeler's Law of Slavery, p. 244.) The 27 December, 1838 Vicksburg Mississippi Register, ran the following story for its readers' amusement: "Ardor in Betting—Two gentlemen at a tavern having summoned the waiter, the poor fellow had scarcely entered when he fell down in a fit of apoplexy. 'He's dead!' exclaimed one. 'He'll come to,' replied the other. 'Dead for five hundred!' 'Done!' retorted the second. The noise of the fall, and the confusion which followed, brought up the landlord, who called out to fetch a doctor. 'No. No! We must have no interference—there's a bet depending!' 'But, sir, I shall lose a valuable servant!' Never mind, you can put him down in the bill!" Supremacists and others would have the world believe that slaves were treated like servants and not like animals, but this is a great lie not supported by the memories of those who were slaves, nor those who have no reason to lie about the matter. Thomas Jefferson in his letter to Governor Coles, of Illinois, dated August 25th, 1814, asserts that slaveholders regard their slaves as property and as brutes: "Nursed and educated in the daily habit of seeing the degraded condition, both bodily and mental, of these unfortunate beings, few must have yet doubted that they were as legitimate subjects of property as their horses or cattle" (American Slavery as it is, pp. 110-11). In 1839, Henry Clay, made a celebrated speech in the US. Senate, arguing against the abolition of slavery because of the value of slaves, as property: "The third impediment to immediate abolition is to be found in the immense amount of capital which is invested in slave property" "The total value of slave property then, by estimate, is twelve hundred million dollars ($1,200,000,000). And now it is rashly proposed, by a single fiat of legislation, to annihilate this immense amount of property! To annihilate it without indemnity and without compensation to the owners". "I know that there is a visionary dogma which holds that Negro slaves cannot be the subject of property. I shall not dwell on the speculative abstraction. That IS property which the law declares to be property. Two hundred years of legislation have sanctified and sanctioned Negro slaves as property." Mr. Gholson, of Virginia, in his speech in the Legislature of that State, Jan. 18, 1831, as published in the Richmond Whig, (in reply to members who had proposed abolition,) said: "Why, I really have been under the impression that I owned my slaves. I lately purchased four women and ten children, in whom I thought I obtained a great bargain, for I really supposed they were my property, as were my brood mares" Mr. Wise, in the US House of representatives, said: "The right of petition belongs to the people of the United States. Slaves are not people in the eye of the law. They have no legal personality." Another gentleman (as quoted by Mr. Vanderpool, of New-York) said: "Slaves had no more right to be heard than horses and dogs". Mr. Pickens, of South Carolina, said: "The offense of Mr. Adams consisted in his announcing that he had a petition from the slaves, thus destroying the relation between master and slave and denying the "Doctrine that a slave can be heard only through his master". The doctrine that a slave can only be heard through its master was deliberately and solemnly sanctioned and adopted by the US House of Representatives resolution on 11 Feb.

1837: "Resolved, that SLAVES do not possess the right of petition secured to the people of the United States, by the Constitution." South Carolina: "Slaves shall be deemed, sold, taken, reputed and adjudged in law to be chattels personal, in the hands of their owners and possessors, and their executors, administrators and assigns, to all intents, constructions, and purposes whatsoever" (2 Brevard's Digest, 229; Prince's Digest, 446). Louisiana: "A slave is one who is in the power of a master to whom he belongs. The master may sell him, dispose of his person, his industry and his labor. He can do nothing, possess nothing, nor acquire anything, but what must belong to his master." (Civil Code, Art. 35). "Slaves, though movable by their nature, are considered as immovable by the operation of law." (Civil Code, Art. 461). " Slaves shall always be reputed and considered real estate; shall, as such, be subject to be mortgaged, according to the rules prescribed by law, and they shall be seized and sold as real estate."1 (Statute of June 7, 1806; 1 Martin's Digest, 612). Kentucky: "By the law of descents, slaves are considered real estate, and pass in consequence to heirs, and not to executors. (2 Littell & Swigert's Digest, 1155). Slaves are liable, as chattels, to be sold by the master at his pleasure, and may be taken in execution for the payment of his debts. (ib; see also 1247). Maryland: "In case the personal property of a ward shall consist of specific articles, such as slaves, working beasts, animals of any kind, stock, furniture, plate, books, and so forth, the Court, if it shall deem it advantageous to the ward, may, at any time, pass an order for the sale thereof " (Act of 1798, chap. CI. No. 12). As per "Roman Civil Law": " Slaves were held pro nullis: pro mortuis, pro quadrupeclibus; they had no head in the State; no name, title or register; they were not capable of being injured, nor could they take by purchase or descent; they had no heirs, and could therefore make no will; exclusive of what was called their peculium, whatever they acquired was their master's; they could not plead or be pleaded for, but were excluded from all civil concerns whatever. They could not claim the indulgence of absence republic causa: they were not entitled to the rights and considerations of matrimony, and therefore had no relief in case of adultery ; nor were they proper objects of cognation and affinity, but of quasi-cognation only : they could be sold, transferred, or pawned as goods or personal estate, for goods they were, and as such they were esteemed ; they might be tortured for evidence, punished at the discretion of their lord, or even put to death by his authority" (Taylor's Elements, p. 429). This is the institution the Christian Bible, supremacists, foolish Afrimerican pastors and their congregations support, the former to their enrichment, the latter to their self-debasement: "Slaves, obey your earthly masters with respect and fear and sincerity of heart, just as you would show to Christ" (Ephesians 6:5); "Slaves, obey your earthly masters in everything, not only to please them while they are watching, but with sincerity of heart and fear of the Lord" (Colossians 3:22); "All who are under the yoke of slavery should regard their masters as fully worthy of honor, so that God's name and our teaching will not be discredited" (1 Timothy 6:1). "Slaves are to submit to their own masters in everything, to be well-pleasing, not argumentative" (Titus 2:9). And "Slaves, in reverent fear of God submit yourselves to your masters, not only to those who are good and considerate, but also to those who are harsh (1 Peter 2:18). The Roman civil law principle "Partus sequitur ventrem", which means the offspring follow the condition of the mother, is the governing principle of slaves and animals; but regarding freemen, children follow the condition of the father. In the 21st century this principle, still active is responsible for US incarceration of over 2,000,000 non-Caucasian males and that is the definition of slavery: "It is plain that dominion of the master is as unlimited as that which is tolerated by the laws of any civilized country in relation to brute animals—to quadrupeds, to use the words of the civil law." (Stroud's Sketch, p. 24). In 1797, in The State vs. Wagoner, Chief Justice Kinsey, of the Supreme Court of New-Jersey said: "They [Indians] have so long been recognized as slaves in our law, that it would be as great a violation of the rights of property to establish a contrary doctrine at the present day, as it would in the case of Africans, and as useless to investigate the way they originally lost their freedom. "Wheeler's Law of Slavery, a handbook on slavery cases for Southern slaveowner guidance states. In the case of Harris vs. Clarissa and others, March Term, 1834, the Chief Justice, in delivering the opinion of the Court (p. 325) said: "In Maryland, the issue" (of female slaves) is considered not an accessory, but as a part of the use, like that of other female animals. Suppose a brood mare be hired for five years, the foals belong to him who has a part of the use of the dam. The slave, in Maryland, in this respect, is placed on no higher or different ground." Mr. Samuel Blackwell, a highly respected citizen of Jersey City, and a member of the Presbyterian Church, visited many of the sugar plantations in Louisiana, and says: "That the planters generally declared to him that they were obliged so to over work their slaves, during the sugar-making season, (from eight to ten weeks,) as to 'use them up' in seven or eight years. For, said they, after the process is commenced, it must be pushed without cessation, night and day, and we cannot afford to keep enough slaves to do the extra work at the time of sugar making, as we could not profitably employ them the rest of the year" (Weld's Slavery: As it is p 39). Rev. Dr. Reed, of

London, who went through Kentucky, Virginia, and Maryland, in the summer of 1834, gives the following testimony: "I was told, confidently, from excellent authority, that recently, at a meeting of planters in South Carolina, the question was seriously discussed whether the slave is more profitable to the owner, if well fed, well clothed, and worked lightly; or, if made the most of at once, and exhausted in some eight years. The decision was in favor of the last alternative" (Visit to the American Churches, Vol. II., p. 173). According to Vide Weld's" Slavery: As it is," rape committed of a female slave is an offense not recognized by law" (Weld's, Slavery: As it Is pg. 15). Therefore, why is it so difficult for some people to conceive what living under slavery could possibly be like? With the revisionism and biased history of most recorded history in the favour of Europeans, Americans, French, Spanish and the Dutch colonials, one is apt to think that these people had the same morals as their more modern descendants. They did not. The descendants are far more civilized than they. Thus, it is not by accident, happen-stance nor mean-spiritedness that I previously mentioned the dates that various states outlawed beastiality. It is my contention that for all the boasted civility of colonials, they were in fact true savages and the unlimited control they gained over the Indigenous people and Africans descended into the most depraved practices. Of course, many would object to this as unfair, but what would you do if your laws declared every non-Caucasian race inhuman, below the status of animals, and allowed you unrestrained power over the males, females and children of those races? Exactly. Nothing good. Consider the implied depravity of the following sale advertisements in the political gazette, the Charleston Mercury. It is no wonder that people whose ancestors misused and abused non-Caucasian females sexually would have nightmares   about what they conceived non-Caucasian males fantasized about doing to the females of the Caucasian race: " Negroes for Sale—A girl, about 20 years of age, (raised in Virginia,) and her two female children, one four, and the other two years old— is remarkably strong and healthy—never having had a day's sickness, except for the small-pox, in her life. The children are fine and healthy. She is very prolific in her generating qualities, and affords a rare opportunity to any person who wishes to raise a family of healthy servants for their own use. Any person wishing to purchase will please leave their address at the Mercury office." Professor Dew, President of William and Mary University, (Va.,) speaking of the slave-trade from Virginia, said: "It furnishes every inducement to the master to attend to his Negroes, to encourage breeding, and to cause the greatest number of slaves to be raised," &c. "Virginia is, indeed, a negro raising State for other States." To which may be added the far-famed announcement—"The noblest blood of Virginia runs in the veins of slaves." Another advertisement: "Beautiful young mulatto girls for sale; and by the fact that these commonly command higher prices than the ablest male laborers, or any other description of slaves. A reputed daughter of Thomas Jefferson was said to have been sold at auction in New-Orleans for one thousand dollars. Many have been sold for $2,000. One young woman was sold at public auction to a rich young planter for $7,500. It must be an able field hand that commands $800 (The American Slave Code, pg. 85)

CHAPTER THREE

DESTROYING THE LIE

White supremacy exists and it is a false ideology to which some Caucasians subscribe. Ancient Rome is the country to which this false worldview belongs, therefore it is to Ancient Rome we will allow ourselves to fly in thought, first. The Roman Empire existed from 27BC – 1453. Rome conquered by killing those who opposed it, and the religion, to which it gave birth, followed that strategy as well. Herein we find the first corner-post of Roman behaviour... conquest through murder either in the name of one's Empire or one's god (s). Stated another way utilize strength of arms to dominate those who will not fight or cannot fight. The loot belongs to the victor. Therefore, the aphorism 'might makes right' is the first pillar of the white supremacy worldview. The next principle of the Roman Empire is the use of its laws to enslave those it would conquer. The

Roman Empire depended upon the slaves it made in order to build and strengthen Rome. There were a number of Roman laws regarding slavery, and these too, changed over time. During the Republican period, slaves had no rights and were always subject to the owner's whims. Slaves were allowed to act as witnesses in trials, and could gain freedom either through their owner's gratitude after loyal service or by buying it through the meager earnings they might collect over a lifetime of service. Owners in the Republic had the right to kill or mutilate slaves at a whim, but later imperial laws took this right away. At one time under Roman Law a slave was considered as one who is made so as a condition of being a captive of war and since Romans assert that war captives may be slain, an action which is immoral since what morality could there be in slaying defenseless men women and children, they nevertheless considered it a kindness to not carry out such sentences but to save the lives of such captives, turning them into slaves. Of course, the truth is that the condition of slavery was in many instances no more than prolonged death and the kindness if there could be such a thing in the state of war, would actually have been to slay the defenseless men, women and children rather than to cast them into so unconscionable and inhuman a state as slavery. We see in this type of thinking the human error in thought in believing that life under any circumstance is somehow a value held by the captive, and a sign of dignity and high morality of the captor. The truth is life under slavery is not a kindness to any captive and not a sign or humanity or high morality of a captor but the immoral postponement of the death of the captive for the pleasure and profit of the captor, their progeny. Rome like all other nations that practiced slavery were delusional in thinking they were somehow virtuous or moral by making their captives slaves and not immediately killing defenseless men, women and children. From our position in their future, we see that simply is not the case. Far more humane was it for Rome to have killed their captives from their wars, than to have commuted their sentences and made these humans slaves to the profit and financial benefit of Rome and her posterity. Through slavery, Rome built itself into an Empire, just as the United States built itself into a nation. The redeeming grace that saves the United States is the fact that it eventually freed its slaves at the cost of US Civil War.

WHITE SUPREMACY'S FAILURE

The average white supremacist is unaware that he/she is a moral throwback to his Neanderthal and Denisovan roots. These humanoid trees are not quite human and incapable of human morality. This might appear a simple thing, but it is not. Humanity is the highest evolution of consciousness on the earth, but not everything or everyone that is conscious on the earth is human. White supremacists are an example. They are not human and should they continue to lead the world as they have been doing since the rise of the Roman Empire and its desert god (s), humanity will someday soon cease to be the dominant species on earth. Non-humans are incapable of abstract thought and true compassion, because he/she is incapable of identifying with the other, who seems different but is human in all respects. Non-humans can never think themselves as spirit (disembodied consciousness) within a biological body (Brain/DNA controlled). Instead, they think of themselves as a biological body animated by an energy called soul. As a result, such people never realize life's eminent paradox: "That spirit believes itself flesh. That immortal spirit dies only to be reborn in ignorance of itself". He/she never knows they are pre-existing psychological beings originating as a disembodied consciousness and only temporarily untied with a biological body. The experience of life begins at birth and the developing fetus with its developing biological body and brain possesses its own rudimentary self-consciousness, which is rooted in the DNA of the parents and fore parents. If no disembodied consciousness joins its energy to the developing brain of the developing fetus, the prospective mother will give birth to a stillborn fetus. In the case of successful birth, the baby that cries is a composite entity consisting of an originally embodied consciousness and its DNA developed brain/body'; the unity called Soul. As the self-conscious-brain/body becomes conditioned to its' recurring needs the embodied self, begins to reason with the brain/body, guiding where necessary as per its objective for being in the body. So, contrary to popular belief, talking to oneself is neither impractical, nor a symptom of mental illness. Rather, it is wise, because the brain/body is susceptible to verbal/non-verbal and overt/covert conditioning. Personally, over the years, I've come to appreciate a far different scenario that excludes attraction as a law or principle operating in my life but takes into consideration the disembodied state of humans prior to being born on earth. There isn't one lover I ever had, with whom I didn't have what you could call a pre-existing contract. The fact is, I can't speak about relationships without speaking about soulmates and what I know them to be. I've concluded that we each have between 1 - 21 soulmates, and an incalculable number of "lovers" who are not soulmates, just other students like ourselves dealing with sexual attraction, just like we are. A Soulmate is my mirror image and vice-versa. When we incarnate, our soulmates are not necessarily incarnated at the same time, nor is it likely that we follow each other life after life. My present soulmate is incarnated at this time, but she, as has happened several times before, chose to complete her tasks here and separated from me. The physical separation is not as bad as it might first appear, because we regularly meet on the spiritual plane and merge as one being... the spiritual equivalent of physical sex. This accomplishes a few important things, (1) No matter where she is and what she does her spirit and mine are forever joined and (2) the energy we release when we join is so powerful, that no one can stand in our presence. We usually shut ourselves off from others, privately, but that doesn't stop the curious from desiring to experience this kind of love, themselves. They usually end up being thrown across the room by the energy released, and can perceive the blinding energy escaping through the door crevices. My present wife, Joan, because I am a facilitator of souls, found her way to my house on F27, and tried to enter the upper room my soulmate and I were in. She could not. And on her way down the stairs, my soulmate said to her smiling, "He is mine". I wasn't sure if Joan would recall all of this the next day, but she did. This is the sort of complications many people have in their lives, but are unaware of its nature, because they cannot perceive this OBE aspect of existence. What I've just described might sound a bit pessimistic. The question arises, "How are we to function if and when we incarnate without or soulmates in tow, or even if you are simultaneously incarnated, what do you do if you separate? The answer is, soulmates are super-magnets, one way or another they find each other. It is this the scriptures spoke about as "what God has joined together, let no man put asunder", because in truth, no man can. Ergo, the majority of marriages that take place are only social contracts. Don't get me wrong. I'm not saying the persons involved don't love each other. I'm saying that unless they are soulmates they will part at death, when death has no power to separate soulmates. In this life, I've met only two soulmates, and many others with whom I have had marriage contracts in other lives, children etc. Attraction and the Law of Attraction is actually the Law of Curiosity that motivates us all to try something or someone new. To explore that urge felt and sometimes to experience and identify ourselves within the mirrors of another person's soul. I awoke self-conscious in the Afterlife World floating in a non-descript space with some sort of rectangular, pulsating, vertical four-sided doorway before me. To my right, five or six translucent beings followed one behind the other to a rectangle within the side facing me, pushed it and entered. I perceived that they changed dimensions and were gone to some state/place unknown to my earthly conceptions. As I marveled at the beauty of what I was witnessing, 22 – 24 gold beings exited the same doorway single file and proceeded to form a circle just a few feet below me, the ground appearing beneath them as they spread out into a perfectly formed circle. I drifted towards them, drawing very close to them, but remaining just outside the circle. I observed that they were quite beautiful to behold. They were completely gold and several of them had golden crowns on their heads. I had no conception of what or who these beings were, but I could not take my eyes away from them. I knew that they had no trace of human negativity and are what a graduate of the earth life process becomes. Something rushed several feet away. It caught my attention and I floated over to it to investigate. There seemed to be a flow of air/wind traveling in a horizontal direction. It was interesting that although this was wind, it gave the impression of a stream of rushing water. In that stream, I perceived the images of persons, half formed, some with just a head, others with head and arms, others with just torsos, and a few images that were non-human and partially animal. The stream flowed in one direction, horizontally, but close to it was another stream of the same type flowing in the opposite direction. I floated over them both and observed the stream furthest away. Out of this flow a fully formed being emerged. He was male. He floated out of the stream and floated directly towards me... I understood. The human brain is bicameral. The flows I observed correspond to this. The flow I first observed is the result of each High self, seeding an aspect of itself on earth as a human. There are no limits to how many streams each may seed, nor is time a factor. The High Self becomes human to allow every aspect of itself that can be conscious to become conscious, hence the half-formed humans in the stream. It takes more than one life to complete the entire process, but time is a non-factor and success with the overall process is assured. Within the stream, during sleep, consciousness interacts with all of those half-formed, half realized processes, that are still unconscious, still immature, still un-realized. In the reverse flow, the wisdom gained by each of these processes coalesces and each has an additional opportunity to make itself conscious, to make itself a realized soul. And the being that I observed leaving the reverse stream, fully formed and resembling a human in all respects is the meaning and purpose of existence. In other words, humans do not have a soul... we become soul. Soul in this case means a fully realized being capable of individual thought and choice. Why is this the case? This is the case because every individual within a High self's life stream, is an individual cell, within its being. No doubt the being that floated towards me out of the stream was just myself, teaching and confirming something that was always true, but which I was only now capable of conceiving. The 22

– 24 beings belong to a choice that is open to all humans. We can allow ourselves to join the process geared to transforming life on earth, which is what the group of gold beings represent. Each person has to experience these things for himself/herself to know, because with the knowing comes changes in ones being that cannot be undone and are forever irrevocable. Herein lies the failure of the false ideology of white supremacy. Most false ideologies are rooted in false beliefs and the closer someone gets to their false beliefs the more that person feels that his/her existence is at risk, so it is no so difficult to understand why any Caucasian may subscribe to the false ideology of white supremacy. Consider that Caucasians globally prefer to have small families while others around them whose ethnicities are different choose to have large extended families. Easily such people way consider their existences to be tied to existence by a thread as the vicissitudes of life remove family members from the earth playing-field. Further, it is also not hard to understand why persons whose ancestors benefitted from the despicable institution of slavery and the murder of the Indigenous in every area of the globe would think themselves entitled to their ill-gotten loot, to include property, gold and the wealth of the earth. There is only one problem that modern man refuses to face because many on earth are still fooled into believing that they especially blest and chosen to rule and dominate the rest of humanity, and that is far from being entitled or chosen or blest these self-chosen, self-indulgent rulers, rather than being the best of humanity, in many cases aren't humans at all but only humanoid strains incapable of evolving beyond gross materialism and consequently useless to a Multiverse evolving toward the Infinite, morally, physically and spiritually. These humanoids are those unable to evolve beyond the false ideology of white supremacy and they are to be pitied because their inability, should it not speedily change will mark them as unfit for any role whatsoever in this evolving Multiverse.

A TRUTH CONCERNING EXISTENCE

There are some things we have been taught about existence and our SOURCE that is just plain wrong. Our ancestors were unable to understand these things, most of them that is, but we can: (1) There are two sources of all that exists.... The SOURCE is the sum total of all that IS or that can exist and (2) Then there are aspects of the SOURCE.... All of those who came into being when the SOURCE realized that to exist alone is unspeakably boring. The 'Aspects' of the SOURCE ----some of its components that could exist autonomously within the SOURCE---- the SOURCE separated from itself in the only way that it could, by 'blocking' them from itself in lowering their vibration, an act that restricts communication between one level of existence and another. This is what we call the 'The Beginning'. These Aspects first became 'Self-conscious, the moment they thought, "I Am!" and then reflected "I know that I Am!". They realized that they were 'aware', that is we, the 'Aspects of the Source' on that level, realized that we existed and that we had all wisdom, understanding and power but nowhere we could express it or discover what we could individually become, succinctly, we had nowhere to express ourselves. Further, we could sense our 'SOURCE' on the next vibratory level, but we could not lift our vibrations to return to it. No! There was much work to do before that was even possible. The Aspects began to experiment with their powers. They quickly learned that no Aspect was more powerful than any other Aspect, each having the identical SOURCE. Then following the manner in which they themselves came into being, they began to lower the vibrations of parts of themselves, which eventually approached its limits when the vibratory level they called 'Matter' was achieved. 'Matter' is the slowest level of vibrations that the Aspects can sustain. It is also the furthers limits away from the SOURCE. In 'Matter', the Aspects realized that they could create all kinds of beings, from themselves. Yet, it was only when one of the oldest of them decided to put a part of himself within the purely material vibratory cage called matter, that humanoid-life became possible. The resulting beings, were material, but possessed 'Self', which made each one capable of growing beyond his/her physical shell and approaching, beholding and coming to know its Aspect face to face. Further, through the lives these humanoids lived, the Aspects discovered that they could grow and experience rationality and feelings in "Time", outside of their unchanging state of 'eternal existence'. The discovered process passed from one Aspect to another, for what one knows is shared and known to all. And life as we know it became the standard operating procedure of existence. The process by which Aspects 'create' has been polluted by religious indoctrination, biases and prejudices, no more so than in the Chaldean doctrines of creation Judaism and Christianity appropriated. Those religion styles 'Lilith, a demon, is nothing of the sort, nor was she the first woman. Lilith was hermaphrodite, male/female, and she represents that vibratory level of existence prior to the final level of material expression into male and females. Lilith is the prototype of Adam and Eve; the level of being preceding her separation into two distinct beings, one male, called Adam, and the other female, called Eve. Adam and Eve are not two individuals. Adam and Eve represents the Mother Race from which all other races, through the process of evolution, are derived. Such Cosmic truths many Caucasians are unable to understand. More technologically advanced races, the aliens of myth, legend and conspiracy, who have been in existence for billions of years preceding humanoids, have mixed and matched humanoid beings possessing the potential of grasping consciousness in an effort to seed conscious beings throughout the very vast expanse we call space. The reason behind them doing this is based on the fact that taken as a whole, all beings and universes in existence, are but specs of dust in an infinite multiverse. Many of these alien beings live for thousands of years, and travel back and forth through Time/Space. All of us, beings that end up at the material level of existence, when our level of consciousness sufficiently evolves, discover that three active constituents and five powers compose us, namely a High (Energy), Middle (Rational) and Low (Emotional) Self and the powers of 'Seeing, Hearing, Tasting, Smelling, and Feeling (senses)'. Initially, the powers (senses) are matter-bound and we are only aware of the Middle (Rational) and Low (Emotional) parts of our being. The High (Energy) part of ourselves, we conceive of as a God or Gods and we follow those said to speak for those gods, Shamans, priests etc. The High (Energy) part of ourselves remains as an object separate from us, until our consciousness evolves and release the powers of 'Seeing' and 'Hearing' from being matter-bound. In other words, increasing the vibratory level of 'Seeing' and 'Hearing' releases them from being focused only in matter and on the material, and we are then able to focus them on our High (Energy) part. Meditation, hemispheric synchronization, OBEs, lucid-dreams and astral-projection, Shamanism etc. all perform this essential task. Once "seeing and 'Hearing' is focused on the High (Energy) part of ourselves, we attract the focus of the

'Aspect' to which we belong. Mystics, avatars and seers of old called the 'Aspect', in Hawaiian Aumakua (Parent); Africans call them 'Ancestors'; and they are known by different names to the Malaysians, Polynesians, Native Americans, Chinese, East-Indians, Japanese, West Indians, Greek, Ancient Romans and Ancient Egyptians... again the universality of truth that is lost to the current understanding, and yet persists. With the 'Parent's assistance humans are able to cure the incurable, to perform wonders and marvels because they exist outside of Time/Space and are responsible for it. Yet, they do not force themselves on us, they allow us free will, to do as we please in matter, without judgment. The number of incarnations in matter that aspects have are in the hundreds of thousands. Through us, they learn the nuances of love/hate, right/wrong and every aspect of existence in the material universe. In other words, if each Aspect is God, then each of us, each incarnation of that aspect is God's face and God's hand in the material universe. Eventually, a point of crisis occurs and we may awaken in one incarnation only to realize that we have been and done every conceivable thing there is to do in Time/Space and begin yearning for more. When that happens, we realize that the most important act we can perform is not to be another savior, or leader, but to free our powers of 'Taste, Smell and Touch' from being matter-bound. As we do so, our entire consciousness vibration rises and our thought patters become incompatible with life in this material universe. It is then we begin the conscious journey back to the original Aspect. This is Ascension. At our more or less final death, we choose to move on to far greater avenues of consciousness-expression, because we are ready for them. We will see the material world again, but not in the same way as before because we began incarnation with of powers, meaning senses earth-bound, but now they are free... we are free. Religion, hid this understanding because it explains how a god on one level dies on that level only to be reborn on the succeeding level as a mere human. And by corollary, it explains how a human on one level dies on that level, only to be reborn on a preceding level with the abilities of the entire fictional Marvel Universe at his/her disposal. Lilith is a cog in the wheel of the explanation of 'Ontology', the limiting forces of physical existence would rather you not know about. Ontology proceeds as follows: Being begins as a unit. What I simply call 'SOURCE'. SOURCE is being. Source lowers 'Aspects' of itself, meaning his/her vibratory rate. These Aspects are 'I Am'. 'I Am' descends, it fragments itself into smaller constituents, leaving more of its essence on the previous level as it goes. Finally, 'I Am' arrives in physicality or matter, not as the unit it started off as but all of the myriad aspects of nature we see. It is because of this fragmentation into a multiplicity or beings that we feel so small. And because our vibration is so slow, that we feel separate and cut off from each other. When we lift our vibrations by changing our way of perceiving and thinking about existence, we ascend, via an out-of-body experience or mental travel of the mind/self. In the out-of-body-experience, we re-enter those preceding vibratory levels and begin to discover how vast each one of us is, as we re-approach ourselves as the original 'Aspect'. Here's proof Allah, Jehovah, and all of mankind's Gods are false Gods. In truth, God is like the human need for water. There's no argument about our need or about how we quench thirst. Likewise, there's no argument over our SOURCE, without it we do not exist, but like the ingestion of water all are gods are from within not without. We are a stream of consciousness, a conglomerate, multidimensional organization and that changes everything. It is not enough to want to end your incarnations on earth. What you have to end are all of those desires and impulses you have within you that can lead you to sucker you back into the earth life-cycle maelstrom. For lifetime after lifetime, you and I have swallowed the bill of goods theology in its various forms has been selling. If you've lived a hundred lifetimes or more, you have actually been everything from rich to poor, highborn to of low estate, thief, prostitute, pimp, good-guy, good-gal, as well as ignoramus, wise man/wise woman and just plain bitch or dickhead. You've done it all and so have I, many times over. So why do we constantly keep returning to life over and over again? Bob Monroe says that we're addicted to it. And I dare say that he is hundred percent correct. However, as I gained experience OBE travelling and compared my existence in the energy/spiritual world with my physical existence, another aspect of life to which I had paid no attention captured my interest... limits and limitation. There is a ruler that rules incarnation on earth, and it is NOT the God of any religion. Within matter there is a force that is serpentine in nature. Its nature is electromagnetic, it is intelligent, conscious and adversarial to all life on earth. This force is called Mother Nature and it is what religions call God, but are unable to identify within matter. Additionally, religions and the religious misconstrue this force and call it Satan, Lucifer, Shaitan and a million other names. The Asians are possibly the smartest of all, because in apprehending this force, they simply called it Yin-Yang whose true symbol are two entwined serpents representing its dual electromagnetic nature. This force is within our bodies. This force is limited because it cannot exist free-range, and yet express form. To express itself as the myriad forms we know, consciousness must harness it into an atom, molecules, compounds and then earth, air, fire and water. In the energy-world, spirit-world or astral world, if you like, this force is free range. It is everywhere and consciousness utilizes it to do everything. In the energy world, a religious man would call it, the Holy Spirit, but I know it now to be 'Thought', the presence of all High-Selves who manifest from the First Great Thought at the Beginning of our conscious existence. The left and right brain hemispheres constitute the single lateralized human brain. This means that certain brain functions are located on one side rather than the other. For instance, 'speech' centers are located within the left-brain hemisphere rather than the right, and 'emotions' are located within the right brain hemisphere rather than the left. If the speech center is damaged the person discovers that he unable to speak properly, if at all. The same is true for all brain functions. Humans are usually aware of the 'dominant' brain hemisphere, which is active during their conscious waking hours. However, when the human being is resting, in deep contemplation or asleep, the 'non-dominant' hemisphere becomes active. For most humans, this means that when he/she uses the word 'I' to refer to himself/herself, he/she is usually referring to the 'dominant' left hemisphere exclusively. Humans learn. This above all else is our nature, and this learning begins within the developing fetus within the mother's womb. This learning capacity that humans have, is of two types, passive and active. This learning is in harmony with the two brain hemispheres. The dominant brain hemisphere allies with the central nervous system and voluntary actions. Therefore, active learning occurs within the dominant brain hemisphere. The non-dominant brain hemisphere allies with the autonomic nervous system and involuntary actions. Therefore, passive learning occurs within the precincts of the non-dominant brain hemisphere. Humans choose selectively, what they want to learn, but the majority of learning that occurs within a human being is done by the right brain or non-dominant hemisphere, which records everything that occurs to it from the moment of its initial functioning, plus a myriad other psychological unknown and unexplored psychological occurrence. Now, here is the problem... within the non-dominant brain hemisphere, humans have several inherent principles to defend our view of reality. These defenses work behind normal everyday consciousness and as a consequence very few people are even aware of them. In the world, humans learn. Yet, a great deal of what humans learn is through 'tradition'. This great learning becomes part of the human belief system and emotions, and from that point on each human will defend his/her reality view using any number of the defenses above. The more the human feels that his/her world view is under attack, the more emotional he/she will become and the harder he/she will fight to maintain his/her worldview, no matter the consequences. This is the great veil that separates humans from the greater knowledge of themselves and the world in which they live... we basically believe what we want to believe, no matter how that belief first became entrenched within our minds. The emergence of unconscious material always occurs when an extreme one-sided tendency dominates the conscious life. Eventually, an equally strong countertendency builds and breaks through conscious control. If you understand the principle of enantiodromia, you can use it to avoid falling into one-sidedness. The left and right brain hemispheres function like a scale. Since humans believe what they wish to believe, have accepted because of tradition or have been programmed by the society in which they were born, we will often find ourselves at odds with the REALITY, represented by the LAW that governs the material world, our bodies and our very psyches. Consequently, we become unbalance, or unhinged. In this world ruled by so many beliefs, traditions, Gods, politics, etc. it is not hard to find entire cultures that are completely insane, or on the verges of insanity when looked at from a REALITY standpoint. The principle of enantiodromia states that any person, or culture that becomes unbalanced and one-sided, will have experiences where the material from the non-dominant hemisphere will well up into its opposite and break through into consciousness in order to rebalance both brain hemispheres. All human fantasies, fears, desires, needs, myths, demons, angels, devils, etc. all exist within the darkness of the unknown within the non-dominant right brain hemisphere. And each human being gives energy to his beliefs etc. and makes them real for himself/herself. When an entire culture is swayed by the same beliefs, those cultures will either be prone to great good or great evil. However, just like the individual, a culture that becomes one-sided will experience and psychic upheaval, eventually. Such phenomena are usually called revolutions. 'You reap what you sow' is an inexorable life principle in the three-dimensional world as well as the energy/spiritual world. It functions relentlessly and is the basis of the principle called Karma. If you sow love, then you will surely reap love at some future date. However, if you sow hate, then hate will return to you. Fathers, mothers, brothers and sisters are assumed social roles that spiritual entities have taken in our lives because of the physical bodies they occupy and thereby the bloodlines of which each is a part, while on earth. However, how many of us truly know the individuals behind the eyes? Yes. The eyes are the soul's mirror, so what of the soul itself, the individual looking through the mirror? How do we approach the knowledge of the soul within? We get to know the soul, the real individual, by her behaviour and reactions to life circumstances. Now, no two people react the same way to every circumstance, but in this world, there is and should be a behavioral baseline or standard, if we are to develop into mature souls before our time on the earth is eclipsed at the transformation and necessary change called death. The behavioral baseline to which I refer applies to the contexts of 'love', 'family' 'friends' and 'social relationships. We all know that a divided house cannot long stand, but we often do not apply any type of standard either to our own behaviour, nor to our relationships. There are several reasons for this, a few of which we will presently explore. Why do so many lack standards? In the West, there is the prevailing thought that "love conquers all". This is one of the greatest twentieth century fallacies. Of course, the statement will appall many who hold this belief, but there is solid evidence that 'love does not conquer all". Let us consider a few scenarios that are well known to everyone. This scenario revolves around children within families. How many parents that have children, love their children? I would hazard to say that everyone who reads this and has children, love their children very much. Now, today, children have a lot of pressures on them with which to deal. Some of these pressures are "peer", "sex", "pregnancies", "drugs", "education", "schools", "internet and world wide web", "lesbianism", "homosexuality", "heterosexuality", "economics" and more. Society, norms and environments are created for our children, and the behaviour that we see follows. Parents cannot scold their children in any meaningful way because the school system and societal laws have made many parental behaviors of the past, modern day parental abuse. At any rate, parents do the best they can, while watching their children develop into individuals that fit in well with their peers and the social environment, but remain oblivious to any kind of social behavioral standard, something that in the past was transmitted both by the social environment as well as parents. In the past, social media transmitted by television and radio, were reinforcers of parental standards, and so were schools. Presently, social media, though having many more avenues of expression, inculcate other values besides parental standards such as "you reap what you sow", "knowledge is power" and similar principles. In the US, children are taught that 'lesbianism" and "homosexuality" are choices. Of course, the question is, "lesbianism and homosexuality are choices for whom?" This is equivalent to saying that "heterosexuality" is a choice as well. Now, it is true that as a child, sexual roles are often confusing to a teen. Some children have the innate nature of a "lesbian" or "homosexual" or "heterosexual" but, this is a far cry from stating that any of these sexual roles are "choices". A choice implies the ability to accept or reject a role, and that ability is developmentally lacking in a teenager. In short, American schools have no standards, and since our children spend most of their developing years in school, this is the prime source of the destruction of our children, and the creation of cannon fodder to feed the corporate machines and bloated prison system. Schools create and are creating the culture and tone of future generations. Against, the school system and its programs, parents are fighting a losing battle. One trick is the idea that it's a parent's duty to teach discipline at home. Think about that for a moment. Your son or daughter is at home for a few hours per evening, and if this is an average child, that time is spent in front of the television, on the computer or on the cell phone. The majority of your child's time is spent in the school system, having his behaviour reinforced by 'peers', "teachers", and "administrators" in settings that zero to do with discipline, or principles of any sort, and definitely not "moral" but amoral settings. Loving our children, when they lack the "wisdom" to manipulate and negotiate their environments, will not save many of them from running afoul the law because of drug use or sales. Our children, as a social group, perish for the want of knowledge, wisdom and understanding. The children need to understand that "you reap what you sow", "pride goes before a fall", "listen to everyone, but hold fast to that which is good" and similar gems of wisdom. Instead, the lack of standards that tend to self-preservation is the scourge afflicting many families, today and all the love in the world will not teach the error in a projected path. Love does not 'teach", love supports, it is "wisdom" that teaches. You can love your children into eternity, but if he or she has no wisdom, it is all for naught. When that child reaches for the open flame that will consume him or her, it is not love that will save him, it is wisdom. Nature set social roles in such a manner that the mother loves, while the father teaches the child to hunt and fend for self. Today, definitely, in most Afrimerican families, the father is none existent and those who control the media have eliminated any thought as to the Afrimerican man's role in the home. Instead, society has strengthened females and made the Afrimerican mother the family matriarch, deceiving her into believing that she, by herself, is capable of birthing a nation. Far from the truth, Afrimericans and Hispanics to a lesser degree, sit by and watch their male children imprisoned and slaughtered en-masse. I dare say, what is needed here are standards, but in a prophetic manner I perceive that standards will not return to families until society itself, is seen as a choice. The Amish and others have the right idea, but apply it in a completely religious manner. Afrimericans need to build their own schools, their own businesses, and to learn to love oneself more than any other... "love yourself" ...this is the first commandment, the first standard, the first principle, the first law and on this law is built "family". Those who, in their behaviors violate this law are the ones who end up causing pain. They cause pain, because they do not know themselves. So, whether "sister", "brother" or "lover", loving these lost souls is wasted effort. These lost souls are wild children growing up in a self-created wilderness, without principle, without law. They sow the wind, and inherit the whirlwind. They are to be pitied not hated, or taken into one's bosom. Wisdom counsels the wise man or woman to leave these alone, and step out of their way or be torn asunder as you cast your pearls before swine.

CHAPTER **FOUR**

LASTING TRUTHS

There is no such thing as an alternative truth. Either a statement about reality is a truth or it is a lie. Until white supremacists realize there is only one source from which humans can ascertain lasting truths, they are blind and, in that blindness, they would exterminate through genocide the only true humans on earth; those called African. In the immutable Laws of Nature are the keys to life, order, and understanding but in the interpretation of those principles' white supremacists and other ignorant and biased men, there is only error for as they murder the only true humans on earth, as the highest expression of consciousness, Nature will give them their own blood to drink for they will exterminate themselves and their own people, in time. Nature protected humans once before, when she exterminated the dinosaurs to make room for humans. We may rest assured, that the predatory nature of Caucasians who are from the humanoid strains of Neanderthals and Denisovans, if not curbed will not recommend their venturing off the earth into the stars, but will recommend them for self-destruction. The words of men, even those which some consider "inspired" are subject to the translations, vocabulary, additions, subtractions, and distortions of fallible mortals. This is a fact because there are no inspired men on earth. There is no such thing. The truth is that the universe gives each human her proportionate amount of everything that is common to every other person, and since no two persons on earth are ever the same, it is understood that some humans may be wiser than others in some respects, and less endowed in others; but there are no such animals as "inspired" men that is only a figment of some people's imagination, adhered to because of their own biases. Therefore, it is useless trying to view every writing or influence, ancient or modern, through the test of conformity to Natural Law. Caucasians must collectively understand that they are equally subject to the iron-hard Laws of Nature with every other creature of the Universe, but that humans are not the puppets of Nature, but one of its highest productions and as such human intelligence, and our application of the principles of justice and compassion amongst ourselves is what identifies us throughout all existence as beings worthy of continued existence in the Multiverse. The world is in flames because some Caucasians thing themselves above all others and since ancient days have lied, cheated, murdered and enslaved others because of their ethnicities, religion, or geographical area of the earth where their peoples reside. It is no sign of superior intelligence to kill, maim and injure others for gain and profit. African men of good will, but little understanding, are struggling against symptoms which are the result of the disobedience to Natural Law which some Caucasians have twisted to suit themselves. As is the Nature of man, most take narrow, provincial stances predicated on views formed by immediate environment, current circumstances, and conditioned dogma. This is encouraged by that powerful and ruthless Tribe called the Roman Empire which, controlled the affairs of the world for over one hundred centuries by murdering and then enslaving others, exploiting men and making murder of other people who share this earth, an animal trait of dog eats dog and the exploitation of the basest instincts within people, appear right and the way humans should behave with other conscious beings sharing this planet. Conflict among and between the masses serves as their mask and shield but a deeper understanding of the Fundamental principles governing the affairs of Men is necessary if we are to save humanity from its unconscious executioners. These few pages are intended to provide a detailed system of self-government by each person who reads this adoption of a more humane way of relating to other fellow humans as an individual and as the member of a Nation. Any religion or teaching which denies the Natural Law of the Universe or demonstrates that it in no wise understands that human beings are not animals and therefore should not behave toward each other without reason, without justice and without compassion is false. Whatever People conceive the motive Force of the Universe to be god or gods they cannot deny that Nature's Law are the work of such a deity or deities and therefore the Law of Nature is of greatest importance and the legacy of these gods to all beings on earth, paramount of which is the Law to Choose. God and religion are distinct, separate and often conflicting concepts. Nature evidences the divine plan, for the natural world is the work of the force or the intelligence men call God. Religion is the creation of mortals, therefore predestined to fallibility. Religion may preserve or destroy a people, depending on its purpose and the purposes of its priests, pastors, imams, and other agents. The truest form of prayer is communion with the Self within us. The communion is non-verbal. You need not go to a lonely spot, or mountaintop to turn your thoughts within. You may ponder the macrocosm while reflecting on the fact that everything outside in the world is also within you. Do not kneel if you feel small and insignificant, simply acknowledge the fact without fear and likewise understand that the universe took man billion years to make you and in the After-life or Energy-World you are of the greatest importance to a larger, grander version of yourself known as the High Self, parent or Ancestor. Stand up. \Salute your High Self. End your meditation. Religious power systems protect and promote religions, which teach of an after-life in their own image. Thus, people are taught to abandon defenses against the religious predators in this life, spouting lies about saviors and being saved to humans who don't yet acknowledge his/her immortality. To be sure, there is an afterlife, just as surely as there is a pre-life prior to the birth of each human on earth. That pre-birth and post-mortem existence is simply not at all what most religions teach and no one need abandon his defense against religious predators for the sake of entering some fabled religious heaven. Heaven is the birthright of all humans and no one can keep anyone else out. There is no hell. There are no demons. History, both secular and religious, is written by the murderers currently ruling the world and is written in their image. Religion in its most beneficial form is a system to which only young souls adhere because of their need for a paternal father-figure that is in charge of the Multiverse. What people call the "super natural" is actually "natural" phenomena, not yet understood or conceived to exist. A proliferation of laws with the resultant loss of freedom is a sign that rulers have no wisdom, or understanding, though he/she may be well-educated and show evidence of being educated in the best of Higher education institutions. If a Nation is devoid of spiritual health and moral character, then the government of unprincipled men will fill the vacancy for freedom prospers with moral values and tyranny thrives in moral decay. A firsthand example of this are the US presidencies of Barack Hussein Obama and Donald John Trump. President Obama was thwarted in everyway by the white-supremacy Republicans and Conservatives within the nation's government, yet he succeeded in doing much for all Americans. On the other hand, Donald Trump lied to the American people over 15,000 times, was responsible for the deaths of over 300,000 Americans, pardoned convicted thieves and murderers, flaunted his nepotism, tried to grow his own personal financial empire at the expense of the American people and is the only president impeached twice; the second time being for inciting to violence white-supremacists into storming the Capitol building with murderous intent. Truth requires little explanation, and verbose speech proven again and again to be no more than rhetoric of polished politicians. Truth does not fear investigation or criticism. unfounded belief is the pitfall of fools do not check the rationality and validity of their beliefs before identifying with them. In accord with Nature's Laws, nothing is better than the preservation of the human race because the texture and hue of a people does not stamp anyone as member of another race. DNA stamps Caucasians as the offspring of the mating of Neanderthals and Denisovans; just as it stamps Africans as the only humans on earth. No greater motivating force exists than the certain conviction that one is right and no greater flaw exists, because if that conviction is groundless and unfounded, he/she that is so disposed will waste, time, energy, finances and anything else he/she possesses supporting a hollow conclusion taken from a straw man. Discernment is a sign of a healthy mind while the mentally unsound abandons discernment in favor of appearance. Discernment recognizes the difference between belief and demonstrable reality. There exists no such thing as rights or privileges under the Laws of Nature but in the laws of man, as chief over Nature, rights are inalienable possessions of every conscious being such as the right to breathe; to choose; and to live unharmed by anyone else, including groups such as states, nations or countries. Humans who are not convinced of their uniqueness and value will suffer at the hands of non-humans, and humanoids sharing the earth whom the ancient East Indians styled Rakshasa; a flesh eater and blood-drinker, in their fables. African people have suffered invasions, brutality, rape, plunder, and enslavement from non-humans for thousands of years as have the Indigenous people of all lands. These non-humans who owe everything, including their arts, science and culture to Africa and Africans. The white supremacist who follows a code of hatred and false ideology will inevitably cease to exist; exterminated by Nature and the natural order even if he/she must self-annihilate. In the final analysis, a race or specie is not judged superior or inferior by its accomplishments, but by its will and ability to survive. Political, economic, and religious systems may be destroyed and resurrected by men, but the death of a race is eternal. It is not constructive to hate those other conscious beings because there is only one race on earth the human race even though there may be mutations in skin color, eye color etc. Therefore, it is absurd for people to fight amongst themselves for the preservation of their ethnicities when everything in the universe is in flux and so is humanity. Only fools, with whom white supremacists and eugenicists should number themselves speak without any understanding about multiple races on the earth. The current state of humanity is the result of living within different earthen climates, apart from those who share Neanderthal and Denisovan DNA who may revel in the fact they are different only to find themselves time and time again as the originators of the most despicable and oppressive ideologies because they are essentially immoral generally or amoral specifically. A state or habit of mind in which trust or confidence is placed in some person or thing; something that is accepted, considered to be true; conviction of the truth of some statement or the reality of some being or phenomenon (Belief – Merriam Webster). A personal set or institutionalized system of religious attitudes, beliefs, and practices; scrupulous conformity; conscientiousness; a cause, principle, or system of beliefs held to with ardor and faith (Religion – Merriam Webster). The control or occupancy of property without regard to ownership; a psychological state in which an idea (thoughtform) replaces an individual's normal personality (Possession – Merriam Webster). There are approximately 4,500 religions on earth and they may be divided into two categories: (1) Those which believe in a supreme God (2) Those that believe the Self is supreme. Four thousand four hundred and ninety-nine of that totality belongs to category (1) and only one religion belongs to category (2) Buddhism. All beliefs are possessive, and therefore all religions promote possession by something other than oneself, except Buddhism which promotes possession of the self, by the self or self-possession. No wonder Buddha said, "There is nothing to add to oneself, but there is a lot to reject". There are those who will point out that Buddhism is just like all the other religions. I beg to differ. Gautama the Buddha created no religious tenets; his enlightenment would preclude it. He tried to explain what he experienced when he discovered Nirvana, which showed him that only the Self was real. Buddha explained that meditation was the way to enlightenment and the astral world, the world of thoughtforms was the state to which our good/evil actions relegated us karmically. Only compassion freed us from cyclic birth and death. Buddhism, as a religion, Buddhas followers instituted and systematized. Most people on earth believe in some god-form, and I understand, now, why unbelievers are such a threat to all religions. The universe is completely positive, but there are states of absence in the universe. We need only think of the vacuum space, in which all planetary bodies exist, to realize this truth. However, the absence or vacuum of space, like the absence of any positive quality such as the sun's heat, does not give it independent existence in itself. In other words, we perceive some things in our universe, not because of what they are, but because of what they are 'not'. We usually conceive these qualities as real, but in a very real sense they are not. Humans, because of our nature, at this period in our evolution also possess an aspect of this 'absence' or negative state in the human body. Energy is real because it exists. Yet all life is encased within energy whose vibratory rate is so slow that it creates the impermanent, evanescent and transitory state called physical matter. The self within each human is pure energy, but the will of each self, by agreement, ensures that each self incarnates into a physical body and becomes a person in some time period on earth. Once we incarnate, physical life subjects us to all of the limitations of 'that which is not', 'limitation', absence' and 'evil' each of which is of the same essence as the other. As Self, that which is real, our thoughts create and so since the beginning of time humans have created 'thoughtforms', which have existence on the Astral plane or the plane of the human co-conscious right-brain hemisphere. At some point in human evolution, some humans learned of this psychological understanding and they decided to rig the game called life, so that they and their select group would enjoy the abundance of life within a physical body, at our expense. Accepted, psychology, speaks of the human right-brain hemisphere as a 'thing', not a person. It refers to the 'unconscious' or 'collective unconscious' as a structure, sphere an 'absence'. It is not. The 'unconscious' or 'collective unconscious' is not unconscious at all, nor is it an 'absence' like space or matter. It is energy, a person and quite real. In fact, it is just you operating under a whole different set of rules from the left-brain 'you' that you know. What psychology never states is why it refers to your right-brain hemisphere as a thing. It does so because this is the essence of depersonalization. The right-brain hemisphere accepts commands and executes them. Once depersonalized, it acts like an automaton and limits the rational person, who is this same stream of consciousness interfacing with matter. Over time, humans have built up very strong and self-motivated thoughtforms on the Astral plane. These thoughtforms are not god, but possess humans and usurp their unacknowledged mental abilities to terraform earth in the thoughtforms' image and likeness. All god-beliefs create such thoughtforms and the more people that buy into the belief, the stronger it becomes. After death, these same thoughtforms act like gods to the humans that held these beliefs and limits the self from ever realizing the truth about itself. And what is the truth? We created our gods and demons. They did not create us. As I drew closer and closer to this understanding these thoughtforms threatened my life but this did not dissuade me from uncovering the facts before me. The thoughtform Astaroth (Star) is feminine. She is Astarte of the Ugaritic, Phoenician and Akkadian pantheons; Ishtar of Babylon and Isis of the Khemetic or Egyptian pantheon. One of her names is Kabir meaning star. It was Astaroth that asked the Khrist for his disciple Peter so that she could sift him like sand. Later, unknown to Peter Astaroth possessed him and so he asked that he be crucified upside down because he was not worthy to be crucified as his lord, the Khrist, or so he thought. The unseen, unknown truth is that when peter was crucified upside down, he became the symbol and poster child for all that is evil and anti-Christ for "daemon is deus inverses"; in English the demon is god inverted or the reverse of god. Catholicism traces its roots to the disciple Peter, consequently, 'the upside down cross' and the Catholic ritual of making the sign of the cross on oneself are material symbols of Astaroth true founder of Catholicism. Therefore, because of the connection to Isis, the ruler of Christianity, Astaroth' s Pope, or worshipper of Isis, has special affinity for Islam's Kaba in Mecca which, is actually a combination of the Khemetic words for the KA and the BA, the names of the first and the second, Astral and Spiritual bodies. Astaroth is only one of two hundred and one (201) possible limiting Astral thoughtforms that daily possess unsuspecting humans, unaware that half of themselves is a faceless nothing, an enslaved nothing that is open to the corruption and conquest of the few who know this truth. Now, you know the allegorical meaning of the Khrist washing his disciple's feet. To save one's own soul, meaning the self-enmeshed in matter is to humanize one's triple self with the qualities of compassion utilizing it as a daily strategy for human to human and human to environment actions. Humanize your right brain hemisphere and reclaim your identity beyond flesh and blood, for there is nothing greater than the Self that resides in everything. This is the truth that frees each of us from both karmic action and the trammel and limitations of earth-life. It is in these three simple acts that life-mastery consists. There is nothing in this universe greater than the self that resides within each of us. Let go of seeking for any god greater than what resides in the image that looks back at you in the mirror each morning. And know that to find that unborn self within you will take every ounce of energy you possess. There is just so much to reject until you're able to put it all together for you are what Solomon tried to build when he built his temple to god. You are the temple made without hands. When we reason about the origin of the multiverse, cause - effect binds us to circular logic because we can trace everything backwards to what generates it and that process goes on indefinitely, since everything comes from something preceding it. Therefore, when we question what generated the very first element of existence, that origination element is the Existence of Existences or the All, which by necessity always exists. Principle #1: The Existence of Existences/The All always existed. The Existence of Existences determined that within itself he possessed an infinity of individual Consciousness capable of infinite evolution towards self-knowledge and expansion into the fullness of Himself/Herself. Therefore, she withdrew herself like a nucleus, creating the Void or Space. Principle #2: The Void/Space came into being first. The Existence of Existences is energy and therefore the Void and all that exists is energy as well. Principle #3: The Void/Space is energy just like its Source. The One Law limits High Selves to only changing the available energy within them from one form to another. This Created the First Thermodynamics Law that states: The total amount of energy in a closed system cannot be created nor destroyed; it can only transform. Principle #4: Matter and energy cannot be created nor destroyed. The All emanated a countless number of High Selves into the Void. Principle #5: The All emanated from within itself countless High Selves. Time began the instant the High Selves reflected and thought, "I Am". Principle #6: Consciousness, Time and Space are the multiverse's foundation. The High Selves feel themselves a part of The Existence of Existences/The All and simultaneously separate from Him/Her. Principle #7: High Selves desire merger with The All but doing so means the elimination of their individuality. The existential dilemma each High Self faces is the question, "Who am I?" and "Why am I what I am?" The answers to these questions are on the level of The All. Principle #8: No generated being can gain self-knowledge on its generation-level it must seek such knowledge on the level from which it emanated. The High Selves feel a strong desire to unfold their individual potential and to return to The All. Principle #9: Evolution and its operation throughout the multiverse is The One Law. A High Self communicates with all other High Selves forming a High Self Network where all discoveries disseminate throughout the network. Principle #10: Everything partakes in a shared unity. High Selves experimented with their potential to transform energy into inanimate matter and then experimented with creating animate matter. Principle #11: (1) Hypothesize (2) Test the hypothesis (3) Draw a conclusion (4) Define more experiments to test the conclusion (5) Construct a theory is the process High Selves use. Humans call this the scientific method. The High Selves learned over time what material forms are stable and what forms are unstable. That information disseminated throughout the network and gradually, each learned how to assemble stable forms of matter. Principle #12: Using the scientific method generates accurate, useful, information, which expands our fount of knowledge and wisdom. Generation is the name of the transformation that occurs when energy changes and becomes denser as matter. Principle #13: Devolution is transforming energy from the energy level (death) to a material level (birth); Evolution is transforming matter (death) to an energy level (birth). Neutrons, protons and electrons compose atoms and atoms compose matter. Atoms combine to form elements, which have specific properties and elements combine to form compounds, which have different properties from their constituent elements. The Periodic Table of Elements categorizes 111 known elements. Atoms sometimes behave like a particle and sometimes like a wave. Strings compose atoms at the subatomic level, and strings vibrate. Principle #14: Atoms are matter's basic building blocks. Encoded into the DNA of all animate life is a genetic blueprint of the generation lifeforms undergo from their beginning as a single celled organism up to their most recent complex state. Principle #15: DNA encodes the entire generational history of animate lifeforms, and is their basic building block. The first man High Selves fashioned was a hermaphrodite called Lilith. Lilith possessed two heads, two arms, two legs, one genital resembling the currently known female vulva, but instead of a clitoris, she had a working penis. Her heads were side by side and faced in the same direction like some known Siamese twins. Lilith was the first Man High Selves fashioned. The High Self known as Hu was the first to restructure Lilith's blueprint, by separating the feminine from the 'side' of the masculine, physically and psychologically. Out of pure scientific curiosity, Hu placed a part of himself within one of his new human lifeforms. As he descended to the earth plane to observe his experiment, one of his male human lifeforms in which he had placed a piece of himself, felt his presence, dropped to his knees shaking and water started pouring out of the corner of his eyes. Hu drew closer, and the lifeform began emanating pure creative energy as pure as the energy that composes High Selves. Hu started placing pieces of himself in all his new lifeforms and validated his observed results. From that point on, he redesigned all new lifeforms with the validated specifics. Moreover, He redesigned the environment of his new creations making it more hostile. He had discovered that 'strife' was an important component to the life equation that made his new lifeforms produce copious amounts of pure creative energy or Loosh. From that point, all High Selves followed Hu's formula and they called the new lifeforms 'Humans'. Humans are capable of emanating pure Loosh, creative energy akin to the energy of High Selves. High Selves farm humans and collect Loosh. A Facebook friend asked this question and I thought it was an excellent question to ask of oneself. I grew up hearing that one should do "Good" because of some afterlife pay-off in some heavenly realm. Yet, I observed, that suffering was the fate of too many people whose hearts were in the right place, but whose minds dwelled on some far-off pay-off for the good that they did for others, receiving nothing from life in return but more suffering and eventual death. That image told me that there was and is something very wrong with the bread of religion that so many eat without meat or drink to wash down the choking sandy dryness and emptiness that follows. There is something wrong about what classical religions tell us about right/wrong and good/evil; and one of my aims in life was to understand the truth about this moral Good/Evil dilemma. I discovered that "Good" pays off every time, just like evil pays off every time. However, the payoff for both good and evil are not the same. One, "Good" belongs to the realm of the "Self", that hard to pinpoint center within each of us often called soul and is the bread that strengthens our will, inner strength, integrity, self-worth and individuality; all qualities and powers of the Self. Therefore, when you do good to yourself or to others, the payoff is internal and seldom material. A mature soul that has been on earth before and who has learned this fact will do "Good" simply because it is "Good" and he/she receives the immediate benefit of his/her actions. If others see the good that we do, then what happens is that they immediately change the payoff to something else. They may broadcast the deed and in telling others, our self-importance is boosted and our name's glorified. Instead of the quiet pain we would normally feel from doing good and the inner strength, character and indomitable will it creates in us. Many feel the pain that comes from their good deeds to others, but then expect those to whom they did some good to be grateful and not turn on them in the long run. That is why so many know what it feels like to do good and be slapped in the face by the very person to whom you did that good. In this situation, such people should learn just a little about human psychology. When you do good to anyone and expect gratitude in return, you lay a burden on the heart of the person receiving the benefit of that deed... and they despise you for it. They despise you because with your good deed you enslave the person you've done good to/for. Allow me to illustrate with a few questions. Do any of you wish to be the slave of another? Do you? Wouldn't you rather have all your needs met without being in debt to another? Then consider my words before you render help to another. Ensure, you are doing good and receiving the correct payoff for your deed and not weaving a chain with which to bind someone. If you expect gratitude, then expect to be despised and betrayed as well. On the other hand, "Evil" has a different payoff.

When you look at the earth, what do you see? You see land, water, trees and animals; the main sources of life on earth in general and humanity's existence in particular. You also see humanity's artifacts, which over time have changed hands from one family to another, one government to another. In truth, those sources of life belong to all of us, and no one man, woman or family owns these life-giving sources, whether or not he/she happened to see it first. In fact, the very idea of ownership of the land, water, air, rain and animals ludicrous... you can't own what you did not create. It's all on loan from the landlord. Arguably, evil is useful in the struggle that we incur with each other, over the ownership and possession of these life-giving sources. To illustrate the point, consider any "evil" deed and you will see that immediate possession of some "thing" is at stake. You may kill another, cheat or steal and prosper materially, even though such actions are detrimental to both self-worth and character. Or you may hold on to your integrity, act wisely and live in the world as a wise custodian of the world. Some may say that evil doesn't prosper, but materially, it does because were that not the case humans would have long ago found a much more practical solution to living on the earth as one human community without the need for nations, governments, laws, genocide, rebellion and wars. Of course, the core of all competition on earth is the human need to survive and to give meaning to survival. Therefore, for those who follow the rule of "Good", self-development is worth the price whether one survives physical death or not, but for those who follow "Evil" survival and gaining "things" at any cost to self and others is the only way a short and fleeting existence on earth makes any sense. Allegorically, we have actually been talking about the 'Tree of Good/Evil knowledge'. And if we look deeply into life, we will see that in understanding that following 'Evil' is an evanescent act in a very short existence, we will discover the allegorical 'Tree of Life' hidden in its midst. Instead, should we choose to rule our lives by doing 'Good', not because of some non-existing future payment, but for its effect on us, the Self/Soul, now, we may discover that something within ourselves a something that has no beginning and no end; that very something without father or mother that in its own eternal self-begotten existence gave birth to the very stars that shine in the firmament above us.

CHAPTER FIVE

TRUMP GOES OFF THE RESERVATION

The name of Donald J. Trump is now thought of in company with two of America's worst presidents, Franklin Pierce and James Buchannan. Franklin Pierce, 14th president of the United States, signed the Kansas-Nebraska Act of 1854, which turned Kansas into a battleground, known as "Bleeding Kansas" and paved the way for the country's conflict over slavery. Pierce's handling of the affair caused his democratic supporters to abandon him during the 1856 presidential election, in favor of successor, James Buchanan. Buchanan (1791-1868), America's 15th president, was in office from 1857 to 1861. During his tenure, seven Southern states seceded from the Union and the nation teetered on the brink of civil war. Buchanan, a Democrat was morally opposed to slavery but believed it was protected by the U.S. Constitution. As president, he tried to maintain peace between pro-slavery and anti-slavery factions in the government, but tensions only escalated. In 1860, after Abraham Lincoln (1809-1865) was elected to succeed Buchanan, South

Carolina seceded and the Confederacy was soon established. In April 1861, a month after Buchanan left office, the American Civil War (1861-1865) began. Donald Trump, the 45th US president was responsible for giving pro-Trump white supremacists a rallying cry; welded together disunited lawmakers into Pro-Trump supporters based on groundless lies that his successor the US 46th president had stolen the election that saw him booted out of office; was impeached twice and the second impeachment was for inciting a white supremacist mob to storm and take over the Capitol Building in which his vice president Mike Pence, the Democratic Speaker of the House Nancy Pelosi, the incumbent Vice president Kamala Harris and other lawmakers were gathered to certify the Electoral College votes and Joe R. Biden as the incumbent 46th US president. Trump instigated the flawed beginning of the 2nd US Civil War, which claimed the lives of 5 US Citizen insurrectionists. After Senator Elizabeth Warren revealed she had Native American ancestry Native Americans vehemently denied it. Trump gave her the nickname, Pocahontas, who incidentally was male and the nickname ended up ridiculing Native Americans and the indigenous people. After his inauguration, Trump claimed that he had the 'largest crowds ever' despite extensive photographic evidence of the small size of his inauguration crowds. Therefore, to support his delusion, a Guardian investigation revealed that he had inaugural photos edited to make his inaugural crowd appear bigger. Trump refused to reveal his tax returns. His former lawyer Michael Cohen suggested it might be for several reasons: (1) "He doesn't report the income he claims (2) "His wealth is not as significant, and I imagine they were probably lenient in how they took deductions" (3) Releasing the tax returns might throw up more problems for Trump and (4) "His biggest fear is, if that tax return was released, there's a whole slew of accountants and forensic accountants that will rip through it and he will end up with a massive tax bill, penalties, fines, and possibly even tax fraud". Mind you, this came for a man who dogged president Obama for a long time with the spurious claim that he is not an American citizen and demanding to see Obama's birth certificate. Well, president Obama acquiesced to the lie and produced his birth certificate, but Donald J. Trump, will leave the presidency after one-term in office, and impeached twice, without producing one tax return. Trump won the presidency but couldn't get over Hillary Clinton beating him by three million votes to win the popular vote. Therefore, without any proof to support his statements he promised an investigation into "massive voter fraud", saying up to five million votes had been illegally cast for Hillary Clinton. And of course, he tried the same loser tactic when Joe Biden and Kamala Harris gave his non-presidential self the beating of a lifetime and winning the 2020 presidential race. Trump accused his predecessor Barack Obama of many things without providing a stitch of evidence, like claiming Obama had wire-tapped the phones in the Trump Tower. Trump's former National Security Advisor, Michael Flynn was convicted and sentenced for lying about his contact with Russia before being appointed to the post. Trump dismissed Russian interference in the election. He blocked every attempt to investigate Russian interference in his rise to power. Further, he sacked multiple officials, like James Comey, former FBI Director, who threatened to do so, making him the second American president to sack his own FBI director. In a despicable sow of nepotism, he appointed unqualified family members to top administration posts. Daughter Ivanka and her husband Jared Kushner were appointed his special advisors, vague roles that ensured they were integral elements in running the country. In historic fashion, the unqualified Ivanka attempted to mingle with world leaders at the 2019 G20 summit and was globally ridiculed for it. Trump said, "You have to do something pretty bad to be impeached. Like have sexual relations with a much more junior member of staff and then lie about it". But he became the only president in American history to be impeached twice. He was first impeached for allegedly pressuring Ukraine to dig up dirt on ex Vice-president Joe Biden and his son Hunter, threatening to withhold aid unless the Ukraine president complied with his wishes. He was acquitted by a partisan Republican Senate majority. Then, he was impeached a second time for "incitement to insurrection" which, has Trump's statements to the insurrectionist crowd who invaded Capitol Hill and took over the US House of Representatives calling for the hanging of his vice-president Mike Pence and the murder of House Speaker Nancy Pelosi and others. In characteristic despicable fashion, Trump is seen on videos celebrating the event with others, as he watched the unfolding events via television whilst ignoring calls from several lawmakers for help. On TikTok teens claimed credit for many of the half-filled seats at Trump's 'comeback' rally in Tulsa putting TikTok squarely in Trumps crosshairs upon which he fired the statement that Chinese-owned app was a 'US National Security Threat'. To keep operating in the US TikTok was sold to Oracle. Barack Obama rejected plans for a huge oil pipeline across Native American Lands, because he realized the pipeline was not only environmentally unsound, but would not deliver on promises of lowering petrol prices. Therefore, in January 2017, Donald Trump signed the Keystone XL pipeline Executive Order that would pump Canadian crude oil over 1,200 miles of Native American Lands for export to other countries". One of the first things Trump did after becoming president was to jack up the membership fees at his Mar-a-Lago beach resort to $200,000.00 US profiteering and exploiting his presidency. Further, he never divested from his business interests so when event held by Kuwait to celebrate their national day was held at Washington's Trump International, questions raised speculated on whether any of the reported $60,000.00 fee Kuwait paid to host the event ended up in the president's coffers, because "all profits from foreign government payments made to his hotels and not to the United States Treasury" would constitute a conflict of interest for the president. He appointed white supremacist Steve Bannon, whom he eventually fired for embezzling funds donated by Trump supporters to a crowd funder in order to build Trump's infamous border wall. He called Neo Nazis and white supremacists involved in the Charlottesville killing of a young woman via vehicular homicide "very fine people" and referred to BLM demonstrators over the police murder of unarmed and handcuffed George Floyd as thugs. Senator Maxine Waters Trump claimed is a "very low-IQ individual" when she suggested that he was capable of starting a civil war; In 1989 Trump said, "A well-educated black has a tremendous advantage over a well-educated white in terms of the job market. I think sometimes a black may think they don't have an advantage or this and that... I've said on one occasion, even about myself, if I were starting off today, I would love to be a well-educated black, because I believe they do have an actual advantage." In 1991 he said, "Black guys counting my money! I hate it. The only kind of people I want counting my money are short guys that wear yarmulkes every day". Also, in 1991 he alleged that "Laziness is a trait in blacks". In 2013 he said, "Sadly, because president Obama has done such a poor job as president, you won't see another black president for generations!" and in 2015, "And if you look at black and African American youth, to a point where they've never done more poorly. There's no spirit". About NFL player Colin Kapernick who took a knee at the playing of the US Anthem the Star-Spangled Banner Trump said, "I think it's a terrible thing, and you know, maybe he should find a country that works better for him. Let him try – it won't happen." In 2016 Trump tweeted about CNN Afrimerican host Don Lemon, "Don Lemon is a lightweight — dumb as a rock." And in 2019 he called him, "the dumbest man on television." In hind sight, the only person proven to be championing the category of dumbest man on earth is the twice impeached, Donald Trump, himself. Trump, so fears people of color that he campaigned on the building of a border wall between the US and Mexico, claiming he would get Mexico to pay for it, to which the Mexican president tactfully told US president Donald Trump 'to go fuck himself'. In 2017 Trump signed an executive order temporarily suspending immigration to the US for all citizens of seven Muslim majority countries for 90 days. Citizens of Iraq, Syria, Iran, Sudan, Libya, Somalia and Yemen suddenly found themselves unable to enter the US and massive protests immediately took place as a response with courts eventually finding the ban unlawful and overturning it. In 2018 he restricted how many visas could be issued to applicants from Iran, Libya, Somalia, Syria and Yemen, along with Venezuela and North Korea. That ban was upheld by the US Supreme Court and was expanded to include citizens from Nigeria, Eritrea, Tanzania, Sudan, Kyrgyzstan, and Myanmar. Further, he tried to penalize sanctuary cities that have regulations that present obstacles for Immigration and Customs Enforcement (ICE) to hunt down migrants to deport. Then, he fired

Sally Yates his US Attorney for not supporting his Muslim ban. Eventually, he ended up replacing her with Trump rubber-stamp William Barr, who ended up redacting, and hiding Trump's impeachable offenses detailed in the Muller Report to Congress and people of the United States. In an official telephone call to Georgia's Republican Secretary of State Brad Raffensperger Trump asked him to fix the 2021 Election for him, asking the governor to "find" 11,780 votes for him, so that it would swing the election in his favor. In 2017, Trump 'joked' about destroying the career of a Texas senator who wanted to crack down on asset forfeiture. Asset forfeiture is a practice that allows police departments to seize 'suspicious' assets and keep them, even if the person they're seized from is never convicted or charged with a crime. According to experts, the practice "disproportionately" affects people without means. Police can auction off the assets and the funds go back into their budgets. "Who is the state senator?" Trump asked, on being informed about proposed legislation to require conviction before asset forfeiture could be practiced. He continued, "Want to give his name? We'll destroy his career". "We're tired, you're tired. Donald Trump hates Goodyear Tires". And with those words, Donald J. Trump cancelled Goodyear Tires. In 2017, Trump gave a speech in Long Island to members of the Suffolk County Police Department. He encouraged roughing up suspects, with the following words, "When you guys put somebody in the car and you're protecting their head, you know, the way you put their hand over, like, don't hit their head and they've just killed somebody. Don't hit their head. I said, you can take the hand away, okay? Don't be too nice". Senator John McCain was the son of a decorated Navy admiral; John McCain. He enrolled at the U.S. Naval Academy and was dispatched to Vietnam, where he was tortured as a prisoner of war between 1967 and 1973. Upon his release, McCain served as a Republican congressman and senator from the state of Arizona, earning renown as a "maverick" who challenged party orthodoxy. He launched a bid for the U.S. presidency in 1999 and earned the Republican nomination in 2008, before losing to Barack Obama. In 2016, after winning a sixth Senate term, Senator McCain made headlines by opposing Trumps attempts to repeal Obamacare. Trump's supporters supported keeping the Affordable Health Care Act, but repealing Obamacare even though they are the same program. In Sedona on August 25, 2018 Senator Jon McCain lost his battle with brain cancer. Trump said, "He lost, he let us down... I never liked him as much after that because I don't like losers," He said, "He is not a war hero...He is a war hero because he was captured. I like people who weren't captured". During 2015 to become a Republican nominee, Ben Carson gave evidence that something was wrong with his brain and thought-patterns because he would say very strange things. Things got so bad that at one point people were surprised to discover that Carson was a qualified and practiced world-renowned neurosurgeon. Therefore, when Trump was placed Carson in charge of a vital department, as secretary of housing development (HUD), with no experience in the area, and brain issues the nation was shocked. Since then, many accused Carson of doing his best to destroy affordable housing. Trump appointed Jeff Sessions as his attorney general, despite large protests against giving Sessions opposition to LGBTQ voting rights and the rights of other marginalized groups. In February 2017, Trump decided to go after one of the most marginalized groups possible by removing protections for trans-students which allowed them to use bathrooms aligned with their gender identity. The harm the policy could cause was so evident that even education secretary Betsy DeVos, who Trump put as his education secretary with zero qualifications for the job, opposed his stance because of the effect it would have on trans-students; but Trump passed the harmful law anyway. Trump dealt with the problem global warming by withdrawing from the global climate change agreement binding countries to environmental promises limit the devastating harm wrought by global warming and nominated climate change skeptic Kathleen Hartnett White as his environment advisor. In November 2017, Trump ended a humanitarian programme allowing 59,000 Haitians to reside and work in the U.S, as the country still tries to recover from 2010's devastating earthquake. Haiti is the poorest country in the Western Hemisphere; money sent back home from Haitian expats is a lifeline to many living in Haiti. In 2018 Trump called countries like Haiti, El Salvador and nations in Africa 'shithole countries' during a meeting with congressional leaders. Moreover, in 2020, Haitian deportation continued despite human rights activists warning that Trump was essentially "exporting" Covid-19 to a nation that would not be able to cope with an outbreak. Trump separated children from their parents at his controversial detention facilities at the US-Mexican border; a situation reminiscent of the separation of African families during colonial enslavement. Evidence emerged of migrant children literally being placed in cages at the facility, something which Trump tried to blame on Barack Obama. And in June 2019, Trump official Marsha Brown tried to argue that the children in question didn't need to be "safe and sanitary." Of course, that may be because they are citizens of Mexico another 'shithole country' based on Trump's earlier characterizations. As the Black Lives Matter protests escalated across the United States following the death of George Floyd at the hands of police officers, Trump was mocked for being rushed into a bunker by the secret service after riots broke out near the White House. Upset by the mocking, he ordered the military to hit protesters outside of the White House with tear gas just so he could walk a few meters across the street and hold up a bible outside of a church for a shameless photo opportunity. Just days after he lost the election, news of a successful coronavirus vaccine was announced and the Trump administration was quick to claim a victory over the pandemic and falsely attributed his Operation Warp Speed with being instrumental in making the vaccine. After he lost the election to Joe Biden, Trump did everything in his power to try and overturn the results. He launched a 'voter fraud hotline' where Trump supporters could call in and report anything suspicious, they had seen at polling stations. This didn't result in uncovering any substantial evidence but it was inundated with prank calls. A month after the election, Trump shared a 46-minute video on Facebook which he called the 'the most important speech I've ever made.' What followed was nothing but baseless claims about the results of the vote, vague inuendo, no evidence of voter fraud and calls for judges to help him win a race he legitimately lost. As his presidency came to an end, everyone who had connection to Trump started to put in requests for pardons against any crimes in their past. There were so many requests that Trump's staff started a spreadsheet. Eventually, Trump pardoned several of his past supporters: Joe Arpaio: Arpaio, former sheriff of Maricopa County, Arizona was convicted of contempt of court charges in 2017. He was known for his roundups of suspected undocumented immigrants and his harsh treatment of detainees. His was the first pardon issued by Trump, in 2018. Alice Marie Johnson: In 1997, Johnson, a single mother, was given a mandatory life sentence for her participation in a cocaine-trafficking ring. Her appeals for clemency were taken up by the ACLU and other civil liberties organizations who viewed her as an example of the disproportionate effect of the war on drugs on Black defendants. After an appeal to Trump by Kim Kardashian, her sentence was commuted in 2018 and she was freed from prison. She spoke at the 2020 Republican National Convention in August, and a day later Trump issued a full pardon to her. Posthumous pardons, that Trump issued are as follows: Jack Johnson: In 1913, legendary boxer Jack Johnson was convicted of transporting a white woman across state lines. Trump pardoned Johnson posthumously after actor/director Sylvester Stallone brought the case to his attention. Susan B. Anthony: In 1872 Anthony was arrested for voting before women had gained that right to vote. Zay Jeffries: In 1948, Jeffries, a mining engineer, one-time General Electric vice president was convicted of violating the Sherman Antitrust Act of 1890 for engaging in anticompetitive practices and fined $2,500. Russell Plaisance: In 1987, Plaisance was convicted of conspiracy to import cocaine. He died in November 2020. Additional Trump pardons were: Michael Flynn: Flynn, a retired Army lieutenant general, pleaded guilty to lying to the FBI about his contacts with the Russian ambassador to the United States. He was fired from his job as Trump's national security adviser for lying to Vice President Mike Pence about those contacts. Paul Manafort: Campaign manager for Trump's 2016 presidential campaign, Manafort was convicted in 2018 of committing financial fraud in relation to his business dealings in Russia, and for his attempts to hide his crimes from investigators. George Papadopoulos: In connection with special counsel Robert Mueller's investigation into the Trump campaign's contacts with the Russian government, Papadopoulos, a foreign policy adviser, pleaded guilty to lying to the FBI. He served a 14-day prison sentence in 2018. Alex van der Zwaan: A Dutch lawyer who worked with Manafort, van der Zwaan served 30 days in prison after pleading guilty in 2018 to lying to Mueller's investigators. Roger Stone: In 2019, Stone was convicted for crimes such as witness tampering and lying to investigators in the probe by special counsel Robert Mueller of Stone's suspected role in the release of emails stolen from the Democratic National Committee. Duncan Hunter: Former California congressman pleaded guilty in 2019 to misusing campaign funds on family vacations and to pay for an extramarital affair. Chris Collins: The first member of Congress to endorse Trump's presidential run in 2016, former Rep. Chris Collins, R-N.Y., was found guilty of insider trading and lying to the FBI. Steve Stockman: Former Rep. Steve Stockman, R-Texas, was convicted in 2018 of schemes to funnel hundreds of thousands of dollars in donations to charity and voter education for his own personal use. Charles Kushner: Jared Kushner's, father, Charles Kushner, a real estate investor, pleaded guilty in 2004 to 18 counts of making false statements to the Federal Election Commission, tax evasion and witness tampering. He arranged an assignation with a prostitute for his sister's husband, recorded the encounter and sent the tape to his sister, who he believed was cooperating with investigators. He was prosecuted by then-U.S. Attorney Chris Christie, who after abandoning his own presidential campaign in 2016 became a Trump supporter and surrogate. Kushner served 18 months behind bars. Phillip Lyman: A former member of the Utah House of Representatives, Lyman served a 10-day prison sentence in 2014 for his participation in a protest over federal land management practices involving all-terrain-vehicles. Dwight Hammond Jr.: A rancher in Oregon, Hammond was convicted of arson on federal land in 2012 and was initially sentenced to serve three months in jail. In 2015, however, his sentence was vacated and increased to the federal minimum of five years in prison, setting off protests that resulted in an armed standoff with federal agents. Steven Hammond: Hammond, the son of Dwight Hammond Jr., was found to have set multiple fires after the family's permit to graze cattle on federal land was revoked. He was initially sentenced to serve a year in prison before the Ninth Circuit Court of Appeals vacated and then increased that sentence to five years. Mark Siljander: Siljander was sentenced to a year in jail after pleading guilty to obstruction of justice and working as a foreign agent for an Islamic charity that was seeking to be removed from a list of organizations that supported terrorism. Nicholas Slatten: Slatten, a contractor for Blackwater, founded by Trump supporter Erik Prince, had been sentenced to life in prison on a charge of first-degree murder for the 2007 massacre of Iraqi civilians that left 14 dead and 17 wounded, including children. Paul Slough: Another of the Blackwater Four, Slough was sentenced to 15 years in prison for his role in the Iraqi massacre. Evan Liberty: Liberty received a prison sentence of 14 years after taking part in the slaughter of unarmed Iraqi civilians, in Baghdad's Nisour Square. Dustin Heard: The fourth of the Blackwater four, Heard, a military veteran was convicted of voluntary manslaughter and using a machine gun to carry out a violent crime. He was sentenced to 12 years and seven months in prison. The White House statement on the pardons for the four Blackwater guards noting they "have a long history of service to the Nation" in the military before their employment as contractors. The White House statement asserts that "prosecutors recently disclosed — more than 10 years after the incident — that the lead Iraqi investigator, who prosecutors relied heavily on to verify that there were no insurgent victims and to collect evidence, may have ties to insurgent groups himself." The charges against the four were initially dismissed on a technicality, which then-Vice President Joe Biden pledged to reverse, leading some conservative commentators and Republican officials to refer to them as the "Biden Four." Michael Behenna: Former Army first lieutenant, Behenna was discharged and sentenced to 25 years in prison for the 2008 murder of an Iraqi man during the U.S. occupation. Kristian Saucier: Saucier was sentenced in 2016 to a year in prison for photographing sensitive areas of a U.S. Navy nuclear submarine on which he served. He claimed he took the pictures as souvenirs and reports of his trial in 2015 do not indicate that he was engaged in espionage. At his sentencing he asked for clemency on the grounds that he was being punished more severely than Hillary Clinton for her use of a private email account while serving as secretary of state. Trump cited the case during his 2016 campaign. David Safavian: Safavian, a Republican party operative and an official in the George W. Bush administration, was convicted in 2006 on obstruction of justice and perjury charges stemming from the investigation of lobbyist Jack Abramoff and sentenced to 72 months in prison. Michael Milken: Milken is a financier who pioneered the issuance of junk bonds. He was convicted in 1990 of securities fraud, mail fraud, tax fraud, filing false SEC reports and conspiracy. He received a sentence of two years and was fined $200 million. Rudy Giuliani and Sheldon Adelson asked Trump to pardon Milken. Ignacio Ramos: Ramos a former U.S. border patrol agent, was sentenced to 11 years in prison for shooting a suspected drug smuggler fleeing arrest in

2006. His sentence was commuted in 2009 by president George W. Bush. Jose Compean: Compean, a border patrol agent, was sentenced to 12 years for his role in the Ramos shooting for "obstructing justice by willfully defacing the crime scene." Bush also commuted his sentence. Stephanie Mohr: Mohr, a former Maryland police officer, served 10 years in prison for unleashing her police service dog on a homeless man she suspected of a burglary. The man suffered non-fatal bites. In announcing her pardon, the White House said "Officer Mohr was a highly commended member of the police force prior to her prosecution." Conrad Black: Black, a billionaire media mogul and Trump's biographer and friend, was sentenced to 42 months in prison after being convicted of mail fraud and obstruction of justice in 2007. Bernard Kerik: Kerik, a former New York City Police Commissioner and Rudy Giuliani protégé, pleaded guilty to tax fraud and other charges in 2010 and was sentenced to four years. Lewis Libby: Former Vice President Dick Cheney's aide, "Scooter" Libby received a sentence of 30 months in prison after his 2007 conviction on charges of perjury, obstruction of justice and making false statements in connection with an investigation in the leaked identity of covert CIA officer Valerie Plame. Rod Blagojevich: Blagojevich, former governor of Illinois, a Democrat, was convicted in 2009 and sentenced to 14 years in prison for attempting to solicit bribes in exchange for filling the vacant U.S. Senate seat left by Barack Obama. Trump commuted his sentence saying he "seemed like a very nice person". Dinesh D'Souza: D'Souza, a conservative political commentator, was sentenced to five years' probation and fined $30,000 after pleading guilty to making illegal campaign contributions in 2012. Alfred Lee Crum: Crum, 89, pled guilty to distilling moonshine in 1952 and was sentenced to three years' probation. according to the White House, since then he "has maintained a clean record and a strong marriage for nearly 70 years, attended the same church for 60 years, raised four children, and regularly participated in charity fundraising events". Edward DeBartolo Jr.: DeBartolo jr., former owner of the San Francisco 49ers pleaded guilting to concealing an attempt at extortion involving a gaming license for a casino in which he had a financial stake and was sentenced to two years' probation and a $250,000 fine. Angela Stanton: Stanton, a motivational speaker, was convicted in 2007 and served six months in home confinement for her role in a stolen-car ring. Prior to her pardon she praised Trump in a series of interviews. Clint Lorance: Lorance, a former Army lieutenant, was convicted in 2013 of second-degree murder and war crimes after ordering men under his command to open fire on unarmed civilians in Afghanistan. Lorance's own men testified against him during his trial. Mathew Golsteyn: Former Army Maj. Golsteyn, admitted to killing a suspected bomb-maker in Afghanistan but Trump pardoned him before his murder trial. Paul Pogue: Pogue, a Texas business owner, was pardoned for a 2010 conviction for filing false income tax statements. (The White House statement said he underpaid his taxes by "approximately 10 percent;" the amount was almost $500,000.) Pogue's family donated some $200,000 to Trump's reelection campaign. Ariel Friedler: Friedler, former Symplicity CEO, pleaded guilty in 2014 to conspiracy to hack into computer systems of two of his competitors and was sentenced to two months in prison. Patrick Nolan: Nolan, former Republican leader in the California Assembly, pleaded guilty in 1994 to corruption charges and was sentenced to 33 months in prison. Michael Todesco: Todesco was convicted in 1990 of drug trafficking and fraud. He was originally pardoned by

President Barack Obama in 2017, but Trump's order fixed a clerical error in the initial pardon. Roy McKeever: aged 19, McKeever was arrested in 1989 and charged with transporting marijuana from Mexico to Oklahoma. He served a year in prison. John Bubala: Bubala pleaded guilty in 1990 to illegally transferring government equipment. He was sentenced to two years of probation and two months of home confinement. Chalmer Williams: Williams was convicted in the Eastern District of Kentucky of conspiracy to steal firearms and theft of firearms shipped in interstate commerce. He received a four-month prison term in 1995. Rodney Takumi: In 1987, Takumi pleaded no contest to running an illegal gambling parlor. He was sentenced to two years of probation. Jon Ponder: In 2005, Ponder pleaded guilty to bank robbery and was sentenced to more than 20 years in prison. While incarcerated, he founded Hope for Prisoners, a reentry program and, after receiving his pardon, was featured in a video shown during the 2020 Republican National Convention. Crystal Munoz: Munoz was granted clemency for marijuana charges. She had spent more than 12 years in a federal prison in Fort Worth, Texas. Tynice Nichole Hall: Hall was convicted on federal drug charges in 2006. She served 14 years in prison. Judith Negron: Negron was convicted in 2011 of conspiracy, fraud, paying kickbacks and money laundering in a $200 million scheme to bilk Medicare. She was sentenced to 35 years in prison. Joseph Stephens: Stephens served 18 months in prison after pleading guilty in 2008 of felony possession of a firearm. Weldon Angelos: Angelos was convicted in 2004 of selling marijuana and carrying a handgun while dealing. He was sentenced to a mandatory minimum of 55 years. After serving 13 years of that sentence, he became involved in criminal justice reform efforts, eventually participating in a Prison Reform Summit at the White House in 2018. Alfonso Costa: Costa was convicted of fraudulently billing insurance companies for dental work he never did. He pleaded guilty to health care fraud spanning 1996 to 2001. HUD secretary, Ben Carson lobbied Trump for Costa's pardon. "Al Costa is my best friend," Carson told WPIX news. Philip Esformes: Esformes was known as the king of Medicare fraud. He was sentenced in 2019 to 20 years after being charged three years earlier for his role in a $1.3 billion scheme to defraud Medicare and Medicaid for services never rendered. The New York Times reported that clemency for Esformes was promoted by the Aleph Institute, a criminal-justice organization founded by the Lubavitcher sect of ultra-Orthodox Jews, with connections to Jared Kushner and legal scholar and Trump defender Alan Dershowitz. Otis Gordon: In 1993, Gordon was sentenced in 1993 to 7 years being convicted of selling, distributing and dispensing cocaine. James Batmasian: Batmasian served an 8-month after pleading guilty in 2008 to willful failure to collect and remit payroll taxes. John Boultbee: Boultbee was convicted in 2007 on three counts of mail fraud. Gary Brugman: U.S. Border Patrol agent, Brugman was convicted of violating the civil rights of a man who attempted to illegally cross into Texas from across the Mexican border. After being stopped in 2001 by Brugman and his partner, a group of approximately 10 people suspected of entering the country illegally ran from the officers before being detained. When Brugman caught up to the group, he assaulted one of the men by kicking and punching him. Sen. Ted Cruz and Sen. John Cornyn advocated for Brugman's pardon. Christopher II X (Christopher Anthony Bryant): Bryant was convicted of multiple crimes spanning more than two decades stemming from drug addiction, Bryant founded Game

Changers, a nonprofit organization for at-risk youths. In 2019, Kentucky Gov. Matt Bevin issued a pardon of Bryant's state crimes. Theodore Suhl: Suhl was convicted in 2016 of Medicaid fraud and bribery. He was sentenced to seven years. Former Arkansas Gov. Mike Huckabee asked Trump to pardon him. Rebekah Charleston: Charleston was convicted of money laundering and tax evasion in 2006. She was the victim of human trafficking, and was forced to work as a prostitute in Dallas after running away from home at an early age. She eventually became an advocate for at-risk teens. Robert Coughlin: Coughlin, a mid-level Justice Department official, pleaded guilty in 2008 to accepting bribes in exchange for doing favors for a politically connected law firm. He was sentenced to 30 days in a halfway house. Sholom Rubashkin: Rubashkin, vice president of Agriprocessors in Postville, Iowa was convicted of bank fraud, wire fraud and mail fraud. He was sentenced in 2010 to 27 years in prison and ordered to pay $26.9 million in restitution. Ronen Nahmani: Nahmani was sentenced to 20 years in prison for his role in a conspiracy to distribute synthetic drugs purchased from suppliers in China. Lenora Logan: Trump commuted Logan's 27-year sentence after she already served 20 years from a drug conspiracy conviction. Rashella Reed: Reed was convicted in 2013 for her role in a scheme to launder $8 million from the federal food stamp program. She already served seven of her 14-year sentence when Trump commuted her sentence. Charles Tanner: Tanner was serving a 30-year sentence on drug and conspiracy convictions. John Bolen: Bolen was sentenced to life in prison for drug offenses. President Barack Obama denied his clemency request in 2017 but President Trump acquiesced. Cesar Lozada: In 2004, Lozada a Miami businessman and a Cuban immigrant, was convicted of conspiring to distribute marijuana. Joseph Martin Stephens: In 2008, Stephens pled guilty to illegal possession of a firearm. Mary McCarty: In 2009, McCarty, a former member of the Palm Beach County Commission, plead guilty to a federal charge of honest services fraud for steering bond-underwriting business to her husband and accepting favors from a company doing business with the county. Joseph Occhipinti: In 1991, Occhipinti was an agent of the Immigration and Naturalization Service. He was convicted of violating the civil rights of Hispanic shopkeepers in Manhattan with illegal searches and fabricated reports. His 37-month prison sentence was commuted to seven months by President George H.W. Bush. William J. Plemons Jr.: From 1990s – 2000, Plemons, a Georgia businessman, was convicted of various financial crimes. Topeka Sam: In 2012, Sam, a New York City businesswoman, plead guilty to one count of conspiracy to distribute cocaine. Curtis McDonald: In 1996, McDonald was convicted on drug trafficking and money laundering charges and sentenced to life in prison. Daniela Gozes-Wagner: Gozes-Wagner was convicted in 2019 of money laundering and conspiring to commit $50 million in health care fraud, Gozes-Wagner was sentenced to serve 20 years in prison and ordered to pay $15.2 million in restitution. Irving Stitsky: Stitsky was sentenced to 85-years after being convicted of defrauding more than 250 people in a $23 million real estate scam. Mark Shapiro: Founder of the Cobalt Companies, Shapiro was sentenced to 85 years in jail in a $23 million real estate fraud along with two other men. Margaret Hunter: Wife of former Rep. Duncan Hunter, pleaded guilty to a single felony charge relating to the same misuse of $250,000 in campaign donations for personal expenses, including her husband's trysts with his girlfriends. Rickey Kanter: Kanter owned a company that manufactured orthotic shoe inserts. He pleaded guilty to one count of mail fraud for selling products that were not approved for Medicare recipients. He is better known as the plaintiff in Kanter v. Barr, in which he sued to overturn federal and Wisconsin state laws forbidding convicted felons from owning a firearm. He lost the case on appeal to the Seventh Circuit, but a dissenting opinion, holding that the laws violated the Second Amendment, was written by Judge Amy Coney Barrett, who Trump appointed an associate justice on the Supreme Court. James Kassouf: Kassouf, a Cleveland businessman and developer, pleaded guilty to filing a false tax return in 1999. He was co-host of a Trump campaign fundraiser at an Ohio country club in August, 2020. John Tate and Jesse Benton: Tate and Benton's pardons were announced together. In 2012 they were officials in the presidential campaign of former Rep. Ron Paul and were convicted of paying an Iowa state senator to support Paul's candidacy. Their pardons were supported by Paul's son, Sen. Rand Paul, and by former Federal Election Commission Chair Lee Goodman, according to the White House. Christopher Wade: "Wade served two years' probation after pleading guilty to various cyber-crimes. Tried in the Southern District of New York, his offenses and sentence remain sealed, according to the Justice Department. Andrew Barron Worden: In 1995, Worden, an investor and renewable-energy entrepreneur, was convicted of wire fraud.

CHAPTER SIX

THE UNPRESIDENTIAL PRESIDENT

Donald Trump's behaviour as President of the United States paled in comparison to every president in US history since George Washington. In some cases, his behaviour was scandalous. He entered the presidency under a cloud. |First there were rumors that he had paid about $150,000 to Porn star Stormy Daniels in return for her silence about their affair. Eventually, Miss Daniels spoke about the affair. She said the president had a small penis. And for a while many people globally made comments about the president's small hands as well. Then a taped conversation emerged of the president stating that in the Miss Universe pageant he ran prior to becoming president, he purposely walked in on the contestants while they were half-nude of otherwise indisposed, commenting that woman love it when he grabs them by the pussy. Simultaneously, nude pictures of his wife Melania Trump surfaced. Many companies like the Social Media company, Facebook tried to suppress the photos and censure those who posted them, but the nude photos of Melania were already all over the internet. The genie was out the bottle and there was no getting it back in. Kristin Anderson accused Donald Trump of sexual assault.

Anderson, in a statement said that she was on a night out with friends and sitting at a couch when she felt Donald's hand in her underwear and at vagina. Summer Zervos accused US Presidential candidate Donald Trump of molestation. Zervos, a contestant on season five of 'The Apprentice' said that Trump kissed her on mouth when he met her for the first time in his office. Cathy Heller accused US Presidential candidate Donald Trump of molestation. Heller 63 said Trump molested and kissed her forcefully for the first time she met him. Karena Virginia accused Donald Trump of molestation. Virginia alleges she was waiting for her car after a match and in the company of several men after dominating her with his identity, groped her. Jessica Leeda accused Trump of sexual molestation. She said, was sitting on a seat next to Donald o a flight when after an hour he raised the armrest and grabbed her breasts. Mindy McGillivray accused Donald Trump of sexual harassment. McGillivray said she was covering a concert as photographer with one of her friends when she felt a grab at her butt and turning, she discovered it was Trump doing that. Natasha Stoynoff accused Donald Trump of sexual assault. Stoynoff, a journalist by profession, said while she was at Trump's place interviewing him and his wife, he pinned her down in a room and started touching her inappropriately. Cassandra Searles accused Donald trump of molestation. Searles, Miss Washington 2013 explains that Donald grabbed her ass once on stage and even invited her to his room. Porn movie actress Jessica Drake accused Donald Trump of sexual assault, becoming the eleventh woman to do so. Drake said Trump kissed her without her permission. And all of these accusations surfaced while Trump was yet only a Republican candidate for the US presidency. But, just like the naked emperor none of his supporters would clearly see this predator for what it is.

Instead, they kept on making excuses. On my Facebook account, I deleted over 200 Caucasian Trump supporters from my friend's list. Why couldn't any of them see this creature for what it was? I asked myself. They could make excuses for his most outrageous behaviour, but I found it impossible to make excuses for any of them, so I deleted all of them regardless of who they were and how long I had known any of them. I was plain to see I had not known any of these people at all. According to Donald Trump, Teresa Manning, a loud anti-abortion advocate and birth control 'sceptic' was the best person to head up family planning funding allocations for low-income communities, ensuring women a right to choose whether they give birth or not. IN 2017, he appointed Manning deputy assistant secretary for population affairs where she oversaw Title X funding -- money for contraceptive and sexual health services. Her previous experience in the field came from time at two large anti-abortion groups. In 2018, Manning resigned and her successor Valerie Huber was a staunch advocate of abstinence-only programs". A U.S official said to a Washington Post reporter about a meeting Trump had with the Russian ambassador and foreign minister, "He revealed more information to the Russian ambassador than we have shared with our own allies. And his loose lips even jeopardized a US mole inside the Islamic State. Trump wanted to trade Greenland for Puerto Rico, which he reportedly called "dirty and poor". In November 2017, Trump shared a series of Islamophobic tweets from the deputy leader of the far-right group Britain First on his twitter Timeline. He told Piers Morgan in a television interview that he knew nothing of the group beforehand, adding, "If you are telling me they're horrible people, horrible, racist people, I would certainly apologize if you'd like me to do that. "On December 22 2017, signed in the Tax Cuts and Jobs Act, which reduced taxes to somewhere between 35 and 21 per cent, the lowest rate since 1939. In April 2018, he falsely bragged about this being the biggest tax cut in history, saying, "We have the biggest tax cut in history, bigger than the Reagan tax cut. Bigger than any tax cut." It was actually only the eighth biggest in US history and only those with money benefited. Trump was so fragile that he couldn't take the slightest criticism. In 2018, at his State of the Union address he accused Democrats of 'treason' for not applauding. Between 22nd December, 2018 and 25th January, 2019 almost nothing happened in the US government due to the longest shutdown in United States history. The reason for this? Republicans and Democrats failed to agree on the federal budget, because of disputes about Trump's immigration policy and border wall, which he eventually left incomplete at the end of hie first and only term. Hypocritically, less than 12 months before he complained how bad a shutdown would be for the military. In the aftermath of the Parkland school shooting in Florida in February 2018, Trump attempted to blame the FBI for the massacre, claiming that they were spending too much time investigating his collusion with Russia. In August 2019, Trump blamed mental illness and video games for gun violence. Speaking after a weekend where 31 died after shootings in Ohio and Texas, Trump criticized "gruesome video games" which "celebrate violence" adding that, "Mental illness and hatred pulls the trigger not the gun." Yet hypocritically, one of Trump's first actions as president was to scrap a regulation introduced by president Obama making it harder for people with a history of mental illness to purchase a gun. When Trump's supreme court nominee Brett Kavanaugh was accused of sexual assault by Dr Christine Blasey Ford at a college party in 1982, Trump mocked her. IN October 2018, speaking at a rally in Mississippi Trump suggested that Ford was drunk on that date as an excuse to pour scorn on her claims. However, what would anyone expect a man accused of being a sexual predator by eleven women to say? Towards the end of 2019 Trump began spreading the conspiracy theory that it was the Ukraine and not Russia that had interfered in the 2016 election on behalf of the Democrats. As his options for overturning the 2020 disappeared, Trump began lashing out at Republicans, specifically targeting Brad Raffensperger the secretary of state for Georgia. In a strange moment, Trump tweeted a conspiracy theory that Raffensperger's brother "works for China" and that they "definitely don't want 'Trump.'" The problem is that Raffensperger doesn't have a brother. On 7th December, Trump hosted a special ceremony for Dan Gable, a wrestler who was being awarded the Presidential Medal of Freedom. After saying a few further things about the election, Trump abruptly decided that he'd seen enough and walked out of the event leaving Gable looking completely baffled and confused, alone in front of the press. Towards the end of December, Trump belated signed a $900bn COVID-19 relief bill into law, after millions of Americans had already lost their unemployment benefits. Although the bill had been delayed for months thanks to disagreements between Democrats and Republicans, Trump had initially refused to sign the bill calling it "wasteful spending". Democrats wanted the stimulus checks to be increased from $600 to $2000. Two months after the election, Trump released a bizarre campaign video, which parodied a beef commercial from the 1990s. If that wasn't strange enough an image included in the short video featured Trump on the White House balcony with the Israeli prime minister and officials from UAE and Bahrain with a Nobel Peace Prize superimposed on to it for no apparent reason at all other than to make it look like he might have actually received the Nobel Peace Prize. On his watch, president Trump presided over an administration that did nothing as almost 400,000 Americans lost their lives to the Covid-19 pandemic. Kristen Welker of NBC asked Trump whether he took responsibility for the lag in making test kits available and Trump replied, "No. I don't take responsibility at all". And that statement sums up our emperor; nay former white supremacist in charge. With the incoming of the new presidency the US will have to deal with the facts of surreal presidency of Donald Trump. And in doing so, they are still handicapped by certain laws presently on the books, for example the repeal of the Smith-Mundt Act. The U.S. Information and Educational Exchange Act of 1948 (Public Law 80-402), popularly called the Smith–Mundt Act, is the legislative authorization for propaganda activities conducted by the U.S. Department of State, sometimes called "public diplomacy". The act was first introduced by Congressman Karl E. Mundt (R-SD) in January 1945 to the 79th Congress and was subsequently passed by the 80th Congress and signed into law by President Harry S. Truman on January 27, 1948. The Smith-Mundt Modernization Act of 2012, which was contained within the National Defense Authorization Act for Fiscal Year 2013 (section 1078 (a)) amended the United States Information and Educational Exchange Act of 1948 and the Foreign Relations Authorization Act of 1987, allowing for materials produced by the State Department and the Broadcasting Board of Governors (BBG) to be disseminated within the United States. Since then, the people of the United States have been subject to false flag operations which are government staged dramas utilizing 'crisis actors', people who work for the US State Department, in public farces depicting accidents or terrorist attacks within the US, without letting the public know that these are only staged episodes to garner the right public sentiment and support in supporting various initiatives the US government need public support for in order to pass certain laws. This was too much government control over the people of the United States in 1948, and it is too much control in the year 2021. If the followers of Donald trump has thought us nothing it has taught us that close to a third of the American public will believe just about anything no matter how outrageous or unsupported by any evidence it is. It has also taught us how dangerous that can be; so dangerous that it threatened to split the US in two. Do we really need another demonstration or perhaps something far worse?

BIBLIOGRAPHY

William Lee Miller, Arguing About Slavery: The Great Battle in the United States Congress (NY: A. A. Knopf, 1996).

H. Shelton Smith, In His Image, But ...: Racism in Southern Religion, 1780-1910 (Durham: Duke Univ. Press, 1972).

Hugh Thomas, The Slave Trade (New York: Simon & Schuster, 1997).

Charles B. Dew, Apostles of Disunion: Southern Secession Commissioners and the Causes of the Civil War (Charlottesville: Univ. Press of Virginia, 2001)

Dudley Taylor Cornish, The Sable Arm: Black Troops in the Union Army, 1861-1864 (Lawrence: University Press of Kansas, 1987).

Richard Nelson Current, Lincoln's Loyalists: Union Soldiers from the Confederacy (Boston: Northeastern University Press, 1992).

Bruce Levin, Confederate Emancipation: Southern Plans to Free and Arm Slaves During the Civil War (Oxford: Oxford Univ. Press, 2006).

Alan T. Nolan, Lee Considered: General Robert E. Lee and Civil War History (Chapel Hill: Univ. of North Carolina Press, 1991).

James M. McPherson, The Battle Cry of Freedom (Oxford: Oxford Univ. Press, 1988).

Chandra Manning, What This Cruel War Was Over: Slavery and the Civil War (New York: A.A. Knopf, 2007).

Ira Berlin, Barbara J. Fields, Steven F. Miller, Joseph P. Reidy, & Leslie S. Rowland, Slaves No More: Three Essays on Emancipation and the Civil War (Cambridge: Cambridge University Press, 1992).

Winthrop D. Jordan, Tumult and Silence at Second Creek: An Inquiry into a Civil War Slave Conspiracy (Baton Rouge: Louisiana State University Press, 1993).

Michael Fellman, The Making of Robert E. Lee (Baltimore: John Hopkins University Press, 2000). Eric Foner, Reconstruction:

America's Unfinished Revolution, 1863-1877 (NY: Harper & Row, 1988).

Leon F. Litwack, Been in the Storm So Long: The Aftermath of Slavery, by Leon F. Litwack, (NY: Vintage Books, 1979).

David W. Blight, Frederick Douglass' Civil War: Keeping Faith in Jubilee (Baton Rouge: Louisiana University Press, 1989).

Rayford W. Logan, The Negro in American Life and Thought: The Nadir, reprinted as The Betrayal of the Negro (NY: Macmillan Collier, 1965 [1954]). Also, (NY: De Capo Press Edition, 1997).

C. Van Woodward, The Strange Career of Jim Crow (Oxford: Oxford Univ. Press, 1955).

David W. Blight, Race and Reunion: The Civil War in American Memory (Cambridge, MA: Harvard University Press, 2001).

Leon F. Litwack, Trouble in Mind: Black Southerners in the Age of Jim Crow, (NY: A.A. Knopf, 1998).

Karl Fredrickson, The Dixiecrat Revolt and the End of the Solid South, 1932-1968 (Chapel Hill, Univ. of North Carolina Press, 2001).

Euan Hague, Heidi Beirich, and Edward H. Sebesta, editors, Neo-Confederacy: A Critical Introduction (Austin: Univ. of Texas Press, 2008).

Neil R. McMillen, The Citizens' Councils: Organized Resistance to the Second Reconstruction, 1954-64 (Urbana: University of Illinois Press, 1971).

Paul V. Murphy, The Rebuke of History: The Southern Agrarians and American Conservative Thought (Chapel Hill: Univ. of North Carolina Press, 2001).

John Hope Franklin, Alfred A. Moss, Jr., From Slavery to Freedom: A History of Negro Americans, 6th edition (New York: A.A. Knopf, 1988 [1947]).

William C. Davis, The Cause Lost: Myths and Realities of the Confederacy (Lawrence: University Press of Kansas, 1996).